C000319710

Axminster .

Discover Devon

www.maverickguide.co.uk

@maverick.guide

EDITOR & DESIGN

Gabriella Dyson

OUR TALENTED TEAM

Editorial Assistant: Rachael Brown

Sub Editors: Amy Kilburn, Sophie Farrah, Colin Everett

Photographers: Matt Austin, Jack Levick, Collette Dyson, Lynsey Taylor, Ali Green

Cover Photo: Clovelly Harbour by Lynsey Taylor

Illustrations: Elin Manon

Special Thanks: Chris Dyson, Chris Onions, Tom Litten, Bob Vanham

GET IN TOUCH

Editorial: editor@maverickguide.co.uk

Advertise with us: partnerships@maverickguide.co.uk

INSTAGRAM

@maverick.guide

@maverick.food

MAVERICKGUIDE.CO.UK

All rights reserved. The Maverick Guide accepts no responsibility for loss or damage of material submitted for publication. The Maverick Guide received written permission for use of photography from each featured business and has made every effort to credit photographers where possible. No part of this publication may be reproduced, copied or transmitted in any form without the written permission.

Printed in England. The Maverick Guide copyright © 2021

Maverick

/mav(ə)rik/ | NOUN

A person who thinks and acts
independently, often behaving
differently from the expected
or usual way.

Hello there!

I'm probably rather biased, but I think Devon is a very special place. It's my home county and for that I count myself very lucky. Its rolling green hills and shingled beaches are the backdrop to my weekends, and for every charming little village - complete with colourful bunting and church fêtes - there are plenty of coastal towns that will give the Algarve a run for its money. In this guide, we uncover some of Devon's hidden gems, as well as the talented artisans and unique experiences it has to offer. So, join us in tossing aside run-of-the-mill handbooks and embrace a whole new kind of travel...

Gabriella Dyson

Editor & Founder

DISCOVER MORE

Burgh Island Hotel

burgh island

Stepping into Burgh Island Hotel feels like a journey back in time - in the best possible way. Set on its own secluded tidal island, this grand hotel was built in 1929 and still boasts its original art deco interiors. It has a fascinating history sprinkled with tales of legendary guests, and each of its twenty five rooms and suites bears the name of a famous visitor.

Adding to the 'Great Gatsby' vibe is the impressive Grand Ballroom - an authentic art deco dining room where tasting menus are accompanied by live piano music and black tie is encouraged. Alternatively, The Nettlefold is a rugged, clifftop restaurant with menus that showcase the freshest, locally caught seafood.

Maverick tip: Book the Agatha Christie Beach House. It offers striking panoramic sea views, a king-size bed, a private sun deck and a hot tub.

Burgh Island Hotel, Bigbury-On-Sea
South Devon, TQ7 4BG

www.burghisland.com

Destination
Plymouth

The city of Plymouth is world-famous for its rich maritime heritage and its popular Plymouth Gin. The historic Barbican district attracts thousands of tourists each year, thanks to its charming, cobbled streets and harbour views, while The Mayflower Steps will forever be known as the spot from which the Pilgrim Fathers set sail for the New World in 1620. Four hundred years later, Plymouth remains a colourful city filled with culture, arts and good hospitality...

Barbican Theatre

Barbican Theatre is a lively cultural hub on Castle Street, focusing on live performance, theatre and comedy from emerging artists. Expect a myriad of exciting acts in its upcoming calendar, from skatepark parkour to laugh-out-loud stand-up gigs at the B-Bar.

Ocean Markets

This celebration of local talent aims to create a fresh take on the market experience. There's a diverse mix of affordable, handmade arts and crafts from regional makers and designers. A trip to Ocean Markets is a great way to support local artists and leave with something unique.

South West SUP, Jay Stone Photography

South West SUP, Tom Godber Photography

South West SUP

South West SUP (above) is situated in the Royal William Yard and offers paddle-board lessons and board hire for the adventurous. Bespoke classes are available for individuals and groups, and we recommend checking out their sunset and full moon paddles. After booking a lesson you're eligible for membership and can join in with their club sessions.

Honky Tonk Wine Library

Honky Tonk Wine Library is one of Plymouth's hidden gems. It's a bit of a hybrid concept, blending together a shop and a wine lounge. Customers are encouraged to sample and purchase wines from around the world and graze on delicious, locally sourced cheese and deli platters. It's a welcoming sanctuary away from the hustle and bustle of the city, where you can sip vino all night and enjoy quality conversation.

Domea Favour

Pronounced "do-me-a favour", this independent chocolate shop was established by self-taught chocolate aficionado, Nicholas Kittle. Everything he sells is handmade and totally unique, often weaving in local produce like Barbican Botanics Gin. Head here for tempting treats like hot chocolate, vegan brownies and handmade truffles.

KUKU

KUKU is an elegant, independent restaurant right in the heart of Plymouth that serves meticulously presented, fresh Japanese cuisine. Plates are colourful and attractive, making the most of local and seasonal ingredients to craft both classic sushi dishes and food with a contemporary twist. Their eye for detail is evident in their cocktails too.

Barbican Kitchen

Established by renowned restaurateurs and TV chefs, James and Chris Tanner, Barbican Kitchen is one of Plymouth's top-rated foodie haunts. Large glass doors slide open to reveal this contemporary restaurant, which offers a menu that is designed to take full advantage of the West Country's larder. Colourful artwork adorns the walls and guests can spy the busy kitchen pass from the comfort of their tables.

Jacka Bakery

Jacka Bakery has become something of an institution amongst Plymouth locals. This could be due to the site's long history of baking (since at least 1610) or it could be their heavenly treats. Warm, freshly baked bread, golden flaky pasties and delicious pastries with egg-yellow custard is the name of the game here. The bakery is also rumoured to be a favoured supplier of Gordon Ramsay, which is praise indeed!

BOX Kitchen & Bar

The Box Kitchen & Bar

With executive chef Nat Tallents at its helm, The Box Kitchen & Bar has been making waves on the Plymouth foodie scene. This bright and airy restaurant celebrates fresh ingredients from the farms, shores and breweries of Devon and Cornwall. The only thing more colourful and exciting than the food is the scenery; you can dine under a fleet of floating figureheads, whose carved faces used to glide across the ocean on the bows of Plymouth ships.

The Fig Tree @ 36

This neighbourhood restaurant is run by a local couple with a passion for good food and hospitality. Taking its name from a fig tree they found in the rear courtyard, the restaurant offers unfussy cuisine that sings of fresh, local produce. The menus change every week and they also offer a fantastic Sunday roast that is worth checking out.

Boringdon Hall Hotel

Plymouth

Boringdon Hall offers a true five-star hotel experience, from its luxe four-poster bedrooms to its award-winning Gaia Spa. This boutique country house is quite possibly the only place in the world where you can sit beneath the stars and sip Champagne from the comfort of a jacuzzi that is positioned within the original turret of an Elizabethan manor!

Boringdon Hall's restaurant, Àclèaf, is a sophisticated and romantic setting, overlooking the original Great Hall. Head chef Scott Paton offers a signature dining experience showcasing inventive British fare, using only the finest, locally sourced ingredients.

Maverick tip: Àclèaf's seasonally-led signature four-course menu is *heavenly*. To complete the dining experience, opt for the paired wine flight, which perfectly matches wines to individual dishes.

Boringdon Hall Hotel, Colebrook
Plymouth, PL7 4DP

www.boringdonhall.co.uk

Gara Rock

east portlemouth

On the South West Coast Path, perched high above rugged smugglers' coves, you'll find Gara Rock. Occupying one of the most enviable vantage points in all of Devon, this boutique hotel has garnered quite the reputation amongst trendy young things. A chic, coastal aesthetic runs throughout the venue, with plenty of melt-into sofas and velvet ottomans to prop your feet on. Floor to ceiling windows offer breathtaking views of the South Devon coast and their one-of-a-kind bedrooms are beautifully kitted out by famed interior designers House Nine.

Gara Rock's restaurant serves a bistro-style menu of simple but delicious food, from tasty crab rolls to gourmet burgers. Alternatively, the relaxed lounge bar offers a wide selection of cocktails, homemade cordials, and local spirits to sip by the fire.

Maverick tip: Why not curl up and watch a movie in the hotel's cinema room? Private screenings can be booked in advance if you'd like to have the screen all to yourselves.

———————————

Gara Rock, East Portlemouth
Salcombe, TQ8 8FA

www.gararock.com

Inner Hope, Photo by Hope Cove House (page 28)

The South Hams

Much of The South Hams is designated as an Area of Outstanding Natural Beauty and its stunning landscape, with all its rivers and rias, coves and creeks, has plenty to appreciate and explore. Amongst the rolling green hills and blue coastal towns, there are exciting pockets of artisan producers, independent shops and passionate makers to discover. Here's what we recommend:

Explore Hope Cove and Thurlestone

In a pretty nook of the South Hams coastline lies Hope Cove and Thurlestone, which are home to a charming collection of pubs and thatched cottages that hug two beautiful sandy beaches. Craft beer lovers will rejoice as The Cove was voted the best in the UK for its selection of hoppy brews. It's also a great place to refuel after a walk along the South West Coast Path or a chilly dip in the sea. Strong swimmers can start at Inner Hope and end at Outer Hope, swimming around a headland and between the two bays.

Eat fresh seafood on the shoreline at The Beachhouse at South Milton Sands

On a sunny day, South Milton Sands is truly glorious. It's perfectly positioned for the golden hour, catching the sun as it hazily sets over the glittering sea and iconic Thurlestone Rock. The Beachhouse is a foodie hotspot that soaks up these views and satisfies all seafood cravings in the process. Although it's a beachside café - and has all the relaxed vibes of one - the price tag is more akin to a typical restaurant. However, the food is so good we're sure you won't mind. With a focus on flavour and quality, you can expect overflowing platters piled high with freshly caught and simply cooked seafood, such as meaty crab claws and plump mussels. Heaven.

Have a riverside foodie experience

Nothing stirs the senses quite like eating and drinking al fresco. Fortunately, Devon is home to plenty of outdoor eateries, including a fabulous riverside experience at the award-winning Sharpham Estate, near Totnes. At their estate and winery, nestled in the beautiful Dart Valley, Sharpham's experienced team offer vineyard tours and guided cheese and wine tastings. These tours give you a chance to savour the fruits of the fields, as you weave your way amongst the vines.

Distil your own gin in Salcombe

If you can find a coveted slot, book a date at Salcombe Distilling Co.'s Gin School, where you can develop and distil your very own 70cl blend of gin. It's a fun, creative experience that lets you get up close and personal with copper pot stills and unique, botanical ingredients. There's something about the waft of salt on the clean air in Salcombe that makes you crave a crisp G&T. So, why not kick back in Salcombe Distilling Co.'s waterside bar and take in the beautiful creek views with a chilled gin and tonic in hand?

Salcombe Distillery's Gin School

Merchants House, Salcombe

Stay in luxurious self-catering accommodation at Merchants House in Salcombe

Merchants House is a gorgeous home-from-home with a contemporary, open-plan layout. Its master bedroom has sensational views of The Salcombe-Kingsbridge Estuary, a lovely en-suite bathroom and a soft king-size bed to collapse onto after a day spent kayaking or milling around Salcombe town. The fully equipped kitchen has all the mod cons you could possibly need for your stay, but there are also private catering options if you'd prefer not to cook (including beach picnics). What's more, a stay at Merchants House means you'll have access to wonderful landscaped gardens with various outdoor seating areas, perfect for al fresco breakfasts or drinks.

Cosy up at a Devon pub that grows its own delicious food

Not often can a pub say that it rears its own sheep, but The Bear & Blacksmith go one step further, managing their own flock. This Chillingdon pub is near obsessive about locally made and sourced produce, maintaining its own vegetable and herb plot and supplying customers with pork, chicken and lamb grown on their South Allington farm. They even have their own butchery, really demonstrating how to master the art of low food miles! The resulting menu is a collection of tried-and-tested classics made with the freshest ingredients, served in a convivial pub atmosphere.

Explore Dittisham

At the point where the River Dart squeezes round a bend, upstream from Dartmouth itself, is the village of Dittisham. Its charm lies in its unspoilt beauty and a sense that it operates outside of normal time. It's also a scenic place for messing about on a boat, and you can rent one from the pontoon in the heart of the bay.

If you prefer to keep your feet on dry land, a pint of traditional ale at the characterful Ferry Boat Inn wouldn't be a bad idea - it's the unmissable, bright pink building - nor would a lunch of fresh crab opposite at The Anchor Stone Café.

Drift down to Bantham on a wild swimming journey

If you're willing to set aside a day for wild swimming, pootle down the estuary on South Devon's River Avon and let the current gently carry you down to sandy Bantham. There's a car park in Aveton Gifford - start here and slide into the river. Enjoy its steady pull as you drift downstream, floating on your back as the landscape passes by you. The sandy riverbed makes for clear waters and a soft ground underfoot. Wearing a wetsuit and boots is best for the walk back, and it goes without saying that you should always consult the tide times before setting off and make sure someone on dry land knows what you're doing.

Enjoy the South Devon surf

Brush up on your surfing, paddleboarding or kayaking on the pristine sandy beach of Bantham, South Devon's most renowned surf spot. Qualified instructors from Bantham Surfing Academy can offer guidance - and patience - taking you up the River Avon on a paddleboard or improving your surfing in a couple of hours. Otherwise, there are boards for hire on the beach. For something a little different, one of their adventure kayak tours will take you to Burgh Island and its many snorkelling coves.

Spend the day in Dartmouth

While Salcombe has its clear blue waters, Dartmouth is arguably the most charming town in South Devon. Its sweeping hillside is covered in colourful houses, leading down to the banks of the River Dart and its many vibrant sailing boats. A trek up to the top of Jawbone Hill offers a beautiful panoramic vista at the top, and when you get back you can finish off the day with a cocktail at Bar 1620 or dinner at Dartmouth's award-winning seafood restaurant, The Seahorse.

Hope Cove House

inner hope

Hope Cove House is an inviting family-run hotel with
stylish and arty interiors on the South Devon coast.
Overlooking the bay of Inner Hope - nestled between
Salcombe to the South and Thurlestone to the North -
few venues are as idyllically located as this.
A theme of white walls and picture windows runs
throughout this bijou hotel, with vibrant pops of colour
introduced via textiles, with light, airy bedrooms offering
views of the gorgeous sandy bay beyond.

The restaurant serves dishes that are seasonal and
coastal, and Hope Cove House is also partial to holding
summer barbecues on their upper terrace. So, you can
fall asleep with a full belly and listen to the sound of
waves lapping in and out of the cove. Bliss.

Maverick tip: The sitting room, bar and restaurant are
open plan. If you would rather not be surrounded by lego
or sticky fingers, book outside of school holidays!

Hope Cove House, Inner Hope
Kingsbridge, TQ7 3HH

www.hopecovehouse.co

Salcombe Harbour Hotel

While we usually champion independents here at Maverick, we're willing to make an exception for Salcombe Harbour Hotel. This 50-room boutique hotel and luxury spa sits right on the shores of the picturesque Salcombe estuary. So, you can step out onto your own private balcony and watch as tiny yachts bob on the turquoise waters below.

The Jetty Restaurant is impeccably designed, with a chic colour palate and a nod to the nautical throughout. The outdoor terrace is the perfect sun trap to enjoy dinner and drinks during the warmer months, while the restaurant itself offers some stunning panoramic views over the estuary. Menus are packed with fresh seafood dishes - such as Jetty Sashimi and steaming bowls of *moules mariniere*.

Maverick tip: The HarSPA is an idyllic place to relax and unwind. Head to the hydrotherapy pool or steam room and make the most of the holistic treatments on offer by premier spa brand Temple Spa.

Salcombe Harbour Hotel, Cliff Road
Salcombe, TQ8 8JH

www.harbourhotels.co.uk/salcombe

Owen Howells Photography

Bowcombe Boathouse

Kingsbridge

Bowcombe Boathouse is an idyllic waterside retreat located in one of the South Hams' most charming towns. What was once the disused storage shed of a traditional Salcombe Yawl, has now been expertly restored in dark teak and aged brass, and decorated with found and foraged materials.

Step inside and you get the sense that the boathouse has been lived in and loved for many years, thanks to the collection of lovingly curated art and artefacts, as well as cosy-luxe furnishings. Today, it's a tranquil space with ever-changing views of the estuary. Curl up by the wood-burning stove or stroll down to the private jetty and kayak into Kingsbridge or nearby Salcombe.

Bowcombe Boathouse, Embankment Road
Kingsbridge, TQ7 4DR

www.bowcombeboathouse.com

Devon Farmhouse

Woodleigh

This Edwardian Farmhouse sits at the heart of a small hamlet on the edge of a 100 acre wood, not far from the traditional market town of Kingsbridge and only a fifteen minute drive from Bantham Beach. The house has a calm, comfortable vibe with elegant, relaxed interiors, stylish detailing and beautiful original artwork throughout. There are four double bedrooms (two en-suite) a further family bathroom, two reception rooms, both with wood burners, kitchen, dining room, cloakroom and boot room.

Throw open the french doors from the kitchen and enjoy brunch in the small, sheltered courtyard under the fig tree or stroll across the lane to your private one acre paddock for rustic dining in the stables, a game of rounders or croquet followed by stargazing around the fire-pit.

Maverick tip:

Right on the doorstep you'll find a 100 acre bluebell wood with walking trails and a babbling brook - perfect for a wild river dip!

———————

Devon Farmhouse, Woodleigh
Kingsbridge, TQ7

www.devon-farmhouse.co.uk

Scot Baston, Cornerstone Photography

Twenty Seven by Jamie Rogers

Kingsbridge

Twenty Seven by Jamie Rogers offers diners a voyage through exciting flavour combinations, dreamt up by one of the most creative chefs in the region. Housed in a former warehouse in the centre of Kingsbridge, the restaurant has gained an enviable reputation for its fine dining credentials and signature presentation. Expect meticulously crafted tasting menus showcasing fine local produce and some pretty stellar drink pairings to compliment your food.

For something extra special, their Willy Wonka inspired afternoon teas are just the *golden* ticket. Three delightful tiers of treats offer sweet, savoury and 'Devonshire' flavours. Whimsical presentation and unexpected combinations are designed to spark the interest of both passionate foodies and casual diners alike.

Maverick tip: They also offer a gourmet takeaway option for homes and holiday rentals within a five mile radius.

———————————

Twenty Seven by Jamie Rogers
9 Mill Street, Kingsbridge, TQ7 1ED

www.27devon.co.uk

Dart Marina Hotel

dartmouth

Sat on the water's edge, on the bank of the Dart Estuary, Dart Marina Hotel is a venue that exudes sophistication. Drawing inspiration from its waterside surroundings, there's a subtle 'yachting chic' vibe to the décor, while large windows offer captivating river views throughout.

Each of the hotel's plush bedrooms and apartments have something unique to offer, be it king size beds with handmade mattresses, coffee machines or binoculars. Upgrade to one of the Junior Suites - with a dual-aspect lounge - or take over a self-catering waterside apartment for a week to remember.

Foodies can choose between fine dining or casual grazing by the riverside, with menus featuring premium local ingredients like ultra-fresh seafood, dry-aged South Devon beef and Sharpham cheeses.

Maverick tip: Throughout the summer you can enjoy drinks and takeaway food from Dart Marina's pop-up vintage 'Cloud Nine' bus on the waterfront.

Dart Marina Hotel, Sandquay Road
Dartmouth, TQ6 9PH

www.dartmarina.com

Rachel Hoile Photography

Josh Campbell Photography

The Angel Taste of Devon

dartmouth

The Angel - Taste of Devon is an absolute treat for lovers of fine dining. Situated in Dartmouth town centre, overlooking the picturesque River Dart, the building itself has a vibrant culinary history. It first opened its doors as The Carved Angel back in 1974 (under famed chef Joyce Molyneux) and quickly became regarded as one of the finest restaurants in the country. Now, reinvented as The Angel - Taste of Devon, head chef Elly Wentworth is at the helm and is doing some pretty extraordinary things.

After bagging a 10/10 for her dessert on the BBC's Great British Menu, it won't come as any surprise that Wentworth is a dab hand in the kitchen. Leading a predominantly female team, she crafts menus that are both accomplished and innovative.

Maverick tip: If you love a G&T you've got to try one made with The Angel's own unique blend of gin. Just make sure you book a table well in advance if you want to secure a spot at this popular restaurant!

The Angel - Taste of Devon
2 South Embankment
Dartmouth, TQ6 9BH

www.theangeldartmouth.co.uk

The Batman's Summerhouse

Kingsbridge

No, not *that* Batman. This cosy cabin was once the 1930s summer house of a military gentleman rather than a caped crusader and is now a hidden gem filled with treasured keepsakes and locally made furniture. Sitting right on the riverbank, it blends into the scenic landscape but there is plenty to do on its doorstep.

Inside, the cabin's interiors have been inspired by family summerhouses in Scandinavia: fresh white walls and grey paintwork, solid wood floors and airy rooms, a personal collection of mid-century furniture and locally made one-offs. There's everything you could possibly need to relax and unwind. Sink into the sofa with a glass of wine or nap outside in the hammock when the sun is out.

Maverick tip: If cooking isn't on the agenda, head to The Sloop Inn, just down the road in Bantham.

———————————

Batman's Summerhouse, Woodleigh
Kingsbridge, TQ7 4DR

instagram.com/batmanssummerhouse

Deborah Schenck Photography

discover
Torquay

'The English Riviera' has earned something of a bad rep in recent years, due in part to its claim to fame as the setting for Faulty Towers and, more recently, car-crash reality show 'The Hotel'. However, despite its dubious television credentials, Torquay's palm-tree-lined streets and blue harbour attract over a million visitors each year. Here's our pick of the best things to do in this famous seaside town:

What's more entertaining than being in a darkened room, warmed by the atmosphere of a laughing crowd, knowing that a reasonably priced bar is onsite? Spend a night with the **Torquay Comedy Club** for a selection of big names and the best local talent from the live comedy circuit.

For a refreshing dip in clear waters, head to **Oddicombe Beach**. It's a stretch of shingle sand, away from the bulk of the crowds, that's linked by a beachside path to **Babbacombe**. Paddle boards and kayaks are available for hire and seals are often spotted around the bay.

On the Rocks is a modern eatery with a laid-back feel and rustic furnishings, overlooking the sands of Torquay beach. When the sun is shining, we recommend sitting outside with a cocktail (obviously). However, if it's a blustery Sunday opt for one of their roasts inside. They're well known for their selection of west country meats and unlimited roast potatoes.

Speaking of good food, **Hamiltons Club** in Babbacombe is another great choice for gourmands. Head here for great quality, contemporary European cuisine and fabulous cocktails in a warm and stylish setting.

Not far from Torquay sit the thatched cottages of Cockington, a quaint countryside village, the centrepiece of which is mansion house **Cockington Court.** Here you'll find a thriving community of artisans, including glassblowers, cider makers, chocolatiers, ateliers and bakers. Wander through the manor grounds, browsing the handmade produce of local craftspeople and chat to them about their trades.

Jodi Hinds Photography

The Elephant Restaurant

torquay

The Elephant Restaurant is the crème de la crème of Torbay's food and drink scene. This bright and informal restaurant offers calming views of Torquay's blue harbour and has enjoyed over fifteen years of Michelin star status thanks to acclaimed chef, Simon Hulstone.

Run by Simon and his wife Katy, The Elephant knows a thing or two about great hospitality. Guests are invited to dine in a laidback, brasserie style space and enjoy fine dining dishes and outstanding tasting menus.

Maverick tip: The Elephant regularly hosts pop-up evenings with talented chefs and rising culinary stars. So, give them a follow on social media to book your spot at their next event!

The Elephant, 3 & 4 Beacon Hill
Torquay, TQ1 2BH

www.elephantrestaurant.co.uk

Riverford Field Kitchen

totnes

Riverford Field Kitchen ticks all the right boxes for us. Organic, plough-to-plate food is the name of the game, with an emphasis on dishes that elevate the humble vegetable. Menus change daily, depending on what's growing in the surrounding fields and polytunnels, and even the most committed carnivores will find themselves in awe of what these guys can do with their five-a-day.

Head Gardener Penny grows a variety of crops for use in the restaurant, such as fresh herbs, radishes, spicy rocket leaves, and fruit for summer puds. Head Chef Lewis Glanvill works creatively with the seasons, crafting delights such as sourdough, ricotta, nettles and pickled wild garlic capers, and pear and gooseberry crumble served with chamomile milk custard. Guests can also dine on the new garden terrace overlooking the gardens.

Maverick tip: Riverford Field Kitchen also offer regular workshops covering everything from bread making to growing your own veg.

———————

Riverford Field Kitchen
Buckfastleigh, TQ11 0JU

fieldkitchen.riverford.co.uk

Totnes

The colourful market town of Totnes is renowned as a magnet for artists, 'alternative types' and London expats seeking the simplicity of rural life...

Totnes High Street is a steep hillside of indie shops and quirky cafes, threading its way up from the River Dart. At the base of the hill sits **The Curator Café** - an intimate coffee shop that showcases the finest wood-roasted coffee and big Italian flavours. Nibble on some handmade biscotti and sip on a perfectly poured flat white as you flick through their curated collection of magazines and vintage books. Upstairs – almost hidden – you'll find **The Curator Kitchen**. Following a similar ethos to below, Italian cuisine is king. The menu changes weekly and reflects the seasons of local South Devon produce. Expect fresh antipasti, delicious homemade pasta dishes and a variety of natural wines.

About halfway up the hill you'll arrive at **Rumour Wine Bar**, a popular haunt that's always packed with locals. Housed in a 14th century building that once served as a toffee factory and a jazz club (though not at the same time), the atmosphere here is warm and the service is relaxed. But it's the food that keeps us coming back. Portions are generous and their Sunday roast packs a real punch.

Totnes Market Square is a thriving hub of activity. Every Friday and Saturday you can catch a busy market, with stalls selling food, clothes, plants and bric-a-brac. Friday is flea market day and if you arrive early enough you can often nab yourself an antique or some pre-loved furniture.

Get your fashion fix at independent retailers **Fifty5a**. Their men's and women's stores are situated side-by-side and their gentlemen's shop has a real rock n' roll vibe to it, with vintage New York inspired interiors and modern classic clothing. Meanwhile, their ladies' shop is dedicated to all things stylish and unique, with beautiful scents and jewellery on display.

A few doors along is **Love Frankie**, a fabulous homeware and interiors shop. Lovers of all things kitsch, they're on a mission to bring a slice of fun back into interior styling, with made-to-order lampshades, eye-popping prints and playful home accessories.

Take a trip back in time at **Totnes Castle.** Managed by English Heritage, this classic Norman motte and bailey castle was founded soon after the conquest to overawe the Saxon town. Climb to the very top of the castle keep and soak in the far-reaching views over the town and across to the River Dart. On a summer's day we recommend bringing your own picnic to enjoy in the grounds under the shelter of its ancient trees.

The Totnes Brewing Co is situated at the bottom of the castle. These guys brew their own craft beers and stock a huge range of guest craft ales and ciders (there's usually about 80 to try). Their beer garden is a great spot from which to take in the castle views, while inside the bar has a warm, rustic vibe that's completed by an open fire on cold days.

Further uphill still is **The Hairy Barista.** You'll have to mind your step on the way, as this coffee shop is a little tight on space. They serve some of the best coffee in town, from aeropress to cold-brew, lattes and espressos.

Love Frankie

A beautifully curated shop brimming with artisan furniture & gifts!

Just a stone's throw from Totnes town is one of our favourite Devon businesses: **Nkuku.** This beautifully curated shop and café is brimming with artisan homewares, as well as handcrafted furniture, Indian antiques and gifts. Borrowing its name from a hut in Zambia, Nkuku works with designers and small businesses from all over the world; with a focus on recycled materials and sustainable production methods. At the heart of Nkuku lies their café, which will welcome you with the aroma of wood-roasted coffee and fresh pastries.

The Hayloft

Ashburton

The Hayloft takes boutique self catering to the next level with sumptuous decor and attention to detail. Housed in a beautifully renovated 17th century hayloft, on the edge of Dartmoor National Park, this self-contained property looks like it's been plucked straight from the pages of 'World of Interiors'.

The well equipped kitchen and dining area has everything you could need to make your own meals, including its very own honesty bar of locally sourced spirits, wines and beers. The rustic wood burning stove will keep you warm during winter, while the secluded terrace is perfect for soaking up the sun during the summer months.

Maverick tip: Sink into the luxurious bateau bath and soak away your stresses, or curl up on the sofa and enjoy a good boxset.

The Hayloft, Western Road
Ashburton, TQ13 7ED

www.thehayloftdevon.co.uk

The Old Library, Ashburton

Visit
Ashburton

The ancient stannary town of Ashburton lies on the southernly edge of Dartmoor National Park. Surrounded by glorious scenery, it's home to an eclectic mix of old and new buildings, as well as an impressive array of antique shops. Its streets are adorned with strings of colourful bunting year-round, and its wall-to wall independent shops and eateries will no doubt tempt you inside...

Taylors is the ultimate destination for 'ladies who lunch'. This thoroughly charming tearoom is one of the town's most popular spots and it's easy to see why. Specialist loose leaf teas command their own menu, and you can choose from a wonderful selection of cakes, cheeses, pâtés and terrines. Treat yourself to a glass of fizz and nibble on bite-sized treats as you catch up with friends.

Ashburton Delicatessen is a treasure trove of independent produce and artisan foods. This modestly sized, family-run deli attracts a stream of loyal customers, who return time and time again thanks to the sights and smells that waft from the kitchen. They stock over thirty different West Country cheeses, along with award-winning charcuterie, locally smoked fish and sweet delicacies like delicate macaroons and fluffy meringues.

A few doors down you'll find **Jaded Palates** – a bottle shop with a difference. Browse their fabulous selection of local spirits and world-class wines, with expert recommendations on hand should you need them.

For evening reservations, try **The Old Library Restaurant**. Run by talented local chefs, Joe Suttie and Amy Mitchell, you'll be treated to a simple yet sophisticated menu showcasing the crème de la crème of local produce. As the name suggests, the restaurant is housed inside a converted library and has bags of homegrown charm to show for it. So, pull up a chair and enjoy dishes such as fresh crab tortellini or twice-baked beetroot and cheese soufflé.

Though 'man shall not live on bread alone', we'd be willing to give it a go if that bread arrived fresh from **Ella Artisan Baker**. This charming little venue is quite possibly the best bakery in all of Devon, so make sure you arrive early, or you might find that they've already sold out of your favourite treats. You've got to try her moreish chocolate rye cookies or a springy loaf of bread fresh from the oven...

The Fish Deli offers an array of fresh seafood and local delicacies, including lobster, River Teign mussels and plump, diver-caught scallops. Owners Nick and Michele both have culinary backgrounds and as a testament to their passion for fresh, sustainable food, they recently published their own fish cookery book. There's also a well-stocked freezer of handmade ready meals.

Bucking the trend of edible offerings, there are plenty of places to go shopping for clothes, accessories and gifts. **Number 30** is your one-stop shop for beautiful second-hand clothes. You can have fun rifling through vintage treasures and come away with a truly unique outfit. **My Fabulous Things** stocks a wonderful selection of women's clothes, accessories and jewellery; while **Tess Designs** is the place to shop for beautiful stationery and gifts.

Take your cookery to the next level

If you want to improve your cookery skills the **Ashburton Cookery School** is the best place to start. With a over 40 cookery courses aimed at home cooks of all levels, you are sure to find a course to enhance your skills and enjoyment of cookery.

Our award-winning courses are taught by experienced chefs using the best ingredients sourced from local producers.

Master a specific skill such as **Knife Skills**, **Patisserie** and **Sauces**, or learn to cook a favourite cuisine on **Italian**, **Mexican**, **French**, **Indian** and **Thai** courses. You can even train to be a professional chef our prestigious Chefs Academy.

View our full range of courses on our website and see how you can take your cookery and home entertaining to the next level.

Ashburton Cookery School & Chefs Academy
Old Exeter Road · Ashburton · Devon · TQ13 7LG · Tel: 01364 652784

www.AshburtonCookerySchool.co.uk

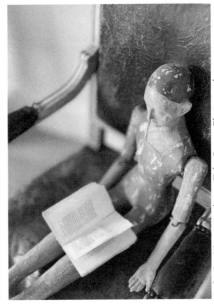

Catherine Waters Antiques, Toby Strong Photography

Ashburton is a mecca for interior designers and antique aficionados. No less than twelve antique and restoration shops line the town's quaint winding streets, offering everything from upcycled furniture to retro reclamation.

Catherine Waters Antiques should be your first port of call if you consider yourself an interior design lover. Catherine has an eye for absurdly beautiful furniture and objet d'art, so you're bound to come away with something seriously chic. Their doors are open Thursday-Saturday, but you can also book appointments at other times.

Alchemy Antiques is another must-visit shop. It's a great spot to look for one-off pieces of furniture to elevate your home. We've fallen in love with a few of their larger items, and if you share our enthusiasm, they're happy to ship worldwide!

You can visit the Ashburton antiques trail website for a comprehensive guide to the town's antique scene: ashburtonantiquestrail.co.uk

Toby Strong Photography

Ashburton Craftmongers

ashburton

Ashburton Craftmongers is a truly magical shop founded by Wildlife Cameraman Toby Strong. Managed and run by local artist Jodi Lou Parkin, the shop is filled from floor to ceiling with a myriad of artisan goods and everyday treasures. Amongst its shelves you'll find hand-woven baskets, ceramics, organic beard oils and wildflower seeds. Everything is lovingly made and assigned to the artist who crafted it. The cherry on top? A portion of Craftmongers' profits go toward supporting a Madagascan school that they built in 2020 called the 'Devon Friendship School '.

Ashburton Craftmongers, 32 North Street
Ashburton, TW13 7QD

www.craftmongers.com

Devon Guild of Craftsmen

bovey tracey

Devon Guild of Craftsmen is an acclaimed exhibition space for contemporary craft and design, as well as a leading charity for craft education. Located in the town of Bovey Tracey – on the edge of Dartmoor – the gallery space and shop host a rotating program of inspiring exhibitions and events. The Guild itself contains over 250 working craftspeople, whose work is regularly showcased onsite.

The Devon Guild shop is the perfect place to pick up a one-of-a-kind item of jewellery, a handmade card or a unique piece of art. They exclusively stock the work of its members, and therefore there's always something original to discover.

Devon Guild of Craftsmen,
Riverside Mill,
Bovey Tracey, TQ13 9AF

www.crafts.org.uk

Art by Takahashi McGil

Moorland View Cottage

north bovey

Moorland View Cottage is quite possibly the most romantic bolthole in all of Devon. Set in the idyllic 13th century thatched village of North Bovey, this charming venue is the perfect cottage for couples looking to get away from it all. Dating from 1704, this former farm labourers' cottage has been decorated in a luxurious, modern rustic style, featuring natural local materials, including ironwork forged by the village blacksmith, Dartmoor sheepskins and hand-turned wooden bowls. Curl up by the log-burning stove, slide into a vintage copper tub for two, or soak up the scenery in the pretty walled rose garden with views of the surrounding countryside.

Maverick tip: Don't fancy cooking? Book your own private fine-dining experience with Harrie Kivell from 'Boo To A Goose'. She'll come to the cottage and serve you a bespoke three-course menu, starting at £100pp.

———————

Moorland View Cottage
North Bovey
Dartmoor, TQ13 8RA

www.moorlandviewcottage.co.uk

Hotel Endsleigh

dartmoor

Hotel Endsleigh is a Grade I Listed country house hotel originally built as a fishing and hunting lodge by the Duke of Bedford in 1814. The hotel is set in a secluded 100 acres of fairytale gardens, woodland, follies and grottos created by Humphry Repton, the last great English landscape designer of the eighteenth century.

In 2004 Olga Polizzi bought Endsleigh and restored it as a luxury hotel, designing the rooms in her inimitable classically elegant English style, with period furniture, contemporary art, roll-top bathtubs, book-lined shelves and squishy sofas to curl up on.

Maverick tip: We *love* Hotel Endsleigh's beautiful afternoon teas, served everyday between 3.30pm and 5pm. We recommend the picnic afternoon tea with Champagne for £37.50.

Hotel Endsleigh, Milton Abbot
Tavistock, PL19 0PQ

www.hotelendsleigh.com

Paul Massey Photography

Gidleigh Park Hotel

chagford

Our stay at Gidleigh Park remains to this day as one of the most impressive experiences we've ever had. This luxurious tudor-style estate is set in over 100 acres of pristine land and offers the sort of good, old-fashioned service that seasoned travels will no doubt expect from a hotel of this calibre.

Gidleigh Park's award-winning restaurant is the perfect spot to celebrate an occasion, offering a fine dining menu, surrounded by Dartmoor's magical beauty. For something extra special, we recommend chef's seasonal tasting menus. There's also a putting course on the grounds, as well as a tennis court, beauty treatments and nature walks to get involved in.

Maverick tip: If you feel like splashing out, book the Dartmeet Suite. It enjoys panoramic views over the valley, with the ultimate decadent bathroom. There's a large marble bath, double shower, steam room and sauna.

Gidleigh Park Hotel, Chagford
Devon, TQ13 8HH

www.gidleigh.co.uk

Southcombe Barn
Midsummer Meadow Bed

dartmoor

For a fairy-tale weekend, it doesn't get much more magical than Midsummer Meadow Bed at Southcombe Barn. Set within an idyllic meadow, this beautiful, hand carved four-poster bed is entirely exposed to the elements; you'll hear the sounds of woodland creatures around you, feel the chill of the night, and wake with the morning dew and birdsong. There's a canopy above the bed which can be left in place or pulled back to reveal the stars of the Dartmoor Dark Sky Reserve as you drift off, and the magic doesn't end there...

A bountiful breakfast is delivered to your open-air bed in a hamper, and each stay includes a half-hour complimentary gong bath to help you drift off even further. There's also a hammock for afternoon naps, a lovely private bathroom up by the barn and a pretty bell tent with daybed.

———————

Southcombe Barn, Widecombe-In-The-Moor
Dartmoor, TQ13 7TU

www.southcombebarn.com

Visit Clovelly

Photography: Lynsey Taylor

A trip to North Devon wouldn't be complete without visiting Clovelly. Often hailed as 'the gem in North Devon's crown', this chocolate-box village hugs the steep cliffside and meanders down to a beautiful historic harbour. Idyllic white-washed cottages, cobbled lanes and colourful fishing boats make this village very photogenic indeed. What's more, there are no cars allowed, so sledges are enlisted to help locals get from A to B...

Mention Clovelly to most people and the first thing that comes to mind are **Clovelly donkeys.** These adorable creatures pulled coaches and carriages up and down the village lanes in the days before motor cars, but today the donkeys enjoy a much more restful existence. You're likely to find them grazing in the meadow at the top of the village, but they're all too happy to pose for photographs!

Clovelly Court Gardens offer quite the contrast to the rustic vibes of the town. Rows of neat, carefully tended gardens are sheltered within its walls and visitors are invited to stroll around its colourful flower beds for a small admission fee. At the heart of the working kitchen garden stands a restored Victorian glasshouse, where you'll find plenty of stone and citrus fruits ripening in the warmth. Outside, there are apple trees, pear trees, quinces, medlars, and even Chinese gooseberries - many of which find their way onto the menus at local pub The Red Lion. During the summer months the bordering flower beds are a riot of colour, and you can keep the memories of your Devon holiday alive by buying bedding plants or herbs from the visitor centre.

There are traces of Clovelly's maritime past everywhere you look, from its cobbled streets to its historical harbour. By 1840, Clovelly was classed as an important North Devon fishing port, with 60 - 70 boats actively working for its herring fishery. Records state that in 1859 'favourable weather' led one local boat to capture nearly 9,000 herring in a one haul - which is pretty impressive when you think about it! Today, you can learn more about the town's proud fishing heritage at **The Fisherman's Cottage**. This unique attraction has been decked out to give visitors an insight into how a Clovelly fisherman and their family would have lived in the 1930s. Step over the threshold to be transported back in time and discover the domestic treasures of a forgotten era. Along with fascinating fishing facts, you can check out old photographs that paint a vivid picture of North Devon in days gone by.

The Clovelly arts and crafts scene is surprisingly vibrant. We're particularly fond of the work of Lydia Jane Duncan, who runs a gallery and studio in the town called **Candyland Studios.** Alongside coastal landscapes, much of the work she creates and showcases follows the theme of British wildlife. It blends together traditional and modern techniques, such as funky lino block prints and colourful, patterned textiles.

There are a handful of places to grab a bite to eat or sink a pint of beer in the village. **The Bay Tree Café** is a popular spot to grab a coffee and a slice of cake. You can sit on the terrace and enjoy the fresh sea air as you take in the amazing views of the North Devon coast and Bideford Bay.

Elsewhere, **The Snug and Harbour Bar** is a cosy inn where you can mingle with villagers and listen to their stories. Few ➡

venues offer such an authentic experience, with solid stone floors, beams, a wood fire and plenty of locals. Every day, fishermen bring their fresh catch to the kitchens, where it is transformed into crab sandwiches, fish finger butties and pies.

Chief among the town's eateries is **The Harbour Restaurant** at The Red Lion Inn. Fresh fish, vegetables and game are delivered from the nearby estate or landed daily right on its doorstep. Feast on famous Clovelly lobsters (when they're in season) and take in the blue harbour views with a glass of wine.

The Red Lion Inn has recently benefited from something of a makeover and now straddles the tricky line of being a historic inn without being too chintzy. It's the perfect spot for a cosy, coastal escape. Try to book a room in 'The Sail Loft', a conversion of an old store next to The Red Lion, that provides six deluxe modern and stylish bedrooms.

You haven't had the full Clovelly experience until you've tucked into an authentic Devonshire cream tea. About halfway down the hill you'll find **The Cottage Tearooms.** On a sunny day its sheltered courtyard is the perfect place to enjoy homemade scones with lashings of clotted cream and jam - just remember it's cream first in Devon!

There's a small admission fee of £8.25pp to visit Clovelly. This might sound as steep as the village itself, but the fee contributes to essential maintenance and upkeep - so it's well worth the price tag.

Ravendere Retreats

ilfracombe

Ravendere Retreats is reinventing the term 'treehouse' with this gorgeous treetop retreat. Sitting snugly under a canopy of mature beech trees, the venue features meticulously designed interiors and a chic decking area. Set in 12 acres of sumptuous woodland - just a couple of miles from Ilfracombe, on the North Devon coast - you'll wake up to gorgeous valley views every morning.

During the warmer months, you can enjoy dinner out on the deck, where a wood-fired pizza oven and a gas barbecue await you. Alternatively, you can keep warm inside thanks to the fully stocked kitchen, irresistible king-size bed, roll-top bath and separate walk-in waterfall shower. Fluffy towels and Korres toiletries are provided to all guests, along with Egyptian cotton towels, bathrobes and luxury bed linens.

Maverick tip: Lee Bay village is a short walk from Ravendere Retreats, along a quiet village road. Enjoy a local Tarka beer at the friendly village pub, The Grampus.

Ravendere Retreats, Lee
Ilfracombe, EX34 8LW

www.ravendere.co.uk

Nick Isden Photography

Lemons Cottage

atherington

At the end of a quiet lane in a quintessential Devonshire village, you'll discover the romance of the picture-postcard, wisteria-clad Lemons Cottage. This Tudor home offers all the comforts and conveniences of the 21st century while retaining its period character.

Push open the solid oak door and discover a downstairs full of original features, an exposed brick fireplace and stone floors. Of course, there's still a thoroughly contemporary vibe to the cottage thanks to its luxurious soft furnishings and mod cons such as superfast fibre broadband, a cinema room, and a baby pink standing bathtub.

Maverick tip: On a sunny morning the garden is perfect for an al fresco brunch, accompanied by birdsong and the gentle babble of the stream.

Lemons Cottage, Atherington
Umberleigh, EX37 9HU

www.lemonscottage.com

The Farmers Arms, Richard Downer Photography

NORTH DEVON FOOD & DRINK

It's estimated that each year over two million tourists visit North Devon, so if you're looking to join them by exiting at Junction 27, take note of these restaurant recommendations by **Chris & Collette Dyson** (aka. the Editor's foodie parents):

THE MASONS ARMS

You don't need to travel far to get to our first venue. Situated just 20 miles up the A361, known as 'The North Devon Link Road,' you'll see signs directing you to the small village of Knowstone, nestled on the edge of Exmoor. Here you'll find The Masons Arms.

This popular restaurant gained a Michelin Star within six months of opening and has held one ever since. Chef Patron, Mark Dobson previously worked at The Waterside Inn in Bray and has some *serious* skills. As you walk into The Masons Arms, you step into the bar - a space with low ceilings and a wonderfully friendly atmosphere; where hikers and dog walkers can sit back and exchange stories around a roaring fire. Meanwhile, the restaurant in the back of the building is modestly-sized and boasts a quirky painted ceiling (think The Sistine Chapel on a micro scale).

The Farmers Arms, Paul Massey Photography

MAIDEN ARCH BY ROBERT BRYANT

Barnstaple is a medieval market town with plenty of character and a variety of shops (if retail therapy is on the agenda). During your visit, you should definitely try to book one the region's newest restaurants: Maiden Arch by Robert Bryant. Bryant aims to provide great food with the ethos that 'the better the food, the less we have to do with it'. Having worked in numerous Michelin-starred restaurants throughout the world, his cooking is pretty special and is made all the better for being back in his hometown.

THE FARMERS ARMS

Further west, on the coastal road near to Bideford, is the small village of Woolsery. Here, together with its fish and chip shop, you'll find The Farmers Arms, which has been subject to a stylish renovation in recent years. Although there are contemporary interiors throughout, the venue still retains its cosy country feel. You can enjoy classic pub fare in the bar area, but we recommend dining in the main restaurant (pictured left) for a more formal experience. A word of warning - the décor is a touch trophy-head heavy in places - but we think the overall aesthetic is fabulous.

NUMBER EIGHT

Heading into the historic port town of Bideford, you'll discover one of the county's top restaurants: Number Eight. Set away on a quiet back street, this small - literally about twenty cover - fine-dining restaurant is perfectly unassuming. It's run by a couple called Chloe and Joshua, who together have years of industry experience under their belts. They use this expertise to offer guests a 7-course tasting menu at each service, that allows the chef to express himself and show the passion that he has for his craft. Booking is absolutely essential if you want to try their food, as the last time we checked there was a two-month waiting list for tables!

RESTAURANT NOEL CORSTON

A great way to build up an appetite is to head along the coastal road, stopping off at Saunton Sands and Croyde Beach along the way. Eventually you'll reach the coastal town of Woolacombe, where you'll find a real hidden gem: Restaurant Noel Corston. Open for dinner reservations only, this is a real bucket list dining experience. Corston offers a single tasting menu sourced largely from the local 'UNESCO Biosphere Reserve'. All diners are served at once, with each course explained to you by Noel and prepared right before your eyes. His lovely wife is also on hand to pour wines and provide drink recommendations.

Number Eight Restaurant, William Reavell Photography

Ellis Parnell picking leaves for dinner at Pyne Arms

Further along the coast is Ilfracombe, a town best known for its beautifully blue harbour, its steep cliffs, and its 20-metre-tall, stainless steel and bronze statue 'Verity' (crafted by famed artist Damien Hirst). The town also boasts two sensational places to eat:

THOMAS CARR 1873

Thomas Carr 1873 is the latest venture for award-winning chef Thomas Carr. He previously ran Thomas Carr at The Olive Room - we promise that's the last time we'll say 'Thomas Carr' in one paragraph - where he earned a coveted Michelin Star. It's testament to the quality and skill of his food that TC 1873 was awarded its own Michelin Star within months of opening - a phenomenal feat achieved by few. The restaurant is situated in Ilfracombe's former police station, close to the harbour, so local fresh line-caught fish and seafood are the focus of many of the dishes.

THE ANTIDOTE

Elsewhere in town is The Antidote. This intimate dining restaurant also offers boutique accommodation in the form of two modern en-suite rooms and a loft style apartment. The restaurant is all about showcasing wholesome food using local ingredients with plenty of flavour. They've been awarded a 'Bib Gourmand' by Michelin and their prices are great value considering the quality.

PYNE ARMS

Finally, if you've packed your hiking boots you're in for a treat. North Devon has an abundance of places to visit that offer scenic walks and trails. If you're joined by your four-legged friend why not try dog-friendly pub and B&B, The Pyne Arms? Set in the picturesque village of East Down on the foothills of Exmoor National Park, this award-winning pub is a popular foodie venue. Dishes are made using locally-sourced and homegrown ingredients and cooked by Chef Proprietor Ellis Parnell. He's joined by his wife Amie at front of house and together they offer guests a wonderful base from which to explore the region.

Paschoe House

Paschoe House is one of Devon's best kept secrets: a country house hotel where classic and contemporary influences blend together harmoniously. Relaxed sophistication is the name of the game, as each of its boutique bedrooms is decorated with designer wall coverings, antique furniture and original artwork. Bathrooms are spacious – many featuring a decadent roll top bath – and the communal areas are thoughtfully designed. The restful morning room, library bar and restaurant all enjoy views across the beautiful landscape and Paschoe House's glorious gardens.

Maverick tip: Paschoe House isn't all about the interiors - it's also a gourmand's dream. We recommend booking the tasting menu in the 3-rosette restaurant.

———————

Paschoe House, Bow
Crediton, EX17 6JT

www.paschoehouse.co.uk

Simon Powell Photography

CIRCA

CIRCA restaurant is located smack bang in the centre of Exeter, making it perfect for date nights and drinks with old friends, as it's right round the corner from the train station. These guys behave as sustainably as possible, championing the farm to fork movement and embracing Devon's seasonal bounty on their menus.

Downstairs is a cosy and contemporary dining space where you can enjoy fine dining dishes, along with a nicely curated wine list. In ordinary times, you'll find their live-music bar upstairs, but in response to the UK lockdown, they've reinvented this space as a farm shop and deli / cafe, showcasing their homemade goods and those of like minded suppliers.

Maverick tip: The cafe is open Wednesay - Saturday 12pm - 4pm, and offers great, locally roasted coffee, sourdough sarnies, cakes and more.

———————

CIRCA, 6 Northernhay Place,
Exeter, EX4 3QJ

circadevon.co.uk

indie Exeter

The historic city of Exeter - known to the Roman's as Isca Dumnoniorum - is widely acknowledged as Devon's cultural capital (we won't tell Plymouth if you don't). From its twisted cobbled streets to its picturesque quayside, there's a myriad of independent businesses and landmarks to explore...

EXETER CATHEDRAL

During your visit, take the rare opportunity to explore one of England's greatest cathedrals and one the finest examples of Gothic architecture in the world. Founded in 1050 AD, construction of a cathedral on the present site began as early as 1114. Inside, Exeter Cathedral's impressive vaulted ceiling is a sight to behold, but to truly appreciate its magnificence you should opt for a rooftop tour - the views over the city are spectacular.

EXETER PHOENIX

Multi-disciplinary art venue 'The Phoenix Centre' connects filmmakers, dancers, DJs, drag performers, musicians and anyone interested in creativity in their hub behind Gandy Street. Pop in for a pint in their bar or terrace before catching live shows, comedy or arthouse films.

THE ROYAL ALBERT MEMORIAL MUSEUM

Whether you've got kids in tow or you're just young at heart, RAMM is fun for the whole family. This world-class museum tells the story of Exeter and Devon from the prehistoric era to the present, along with interactive exhibits and a beautifully curated gift shop. On a rainy day this should be your first stop!

TOPSHAM BREWERY

This microbrewery and tap house is one of the hottest spots for music in town. On summer nights, you can take a seat on the historic quayside and listen to live performances under the twinkling lights, with a craft beer in hand.

FORE STREET FLEA MARKET

Look out for this monthly gathering of local artisans, selling everything from handmade ceramics to macramé wall hangings. For details of their next event keep your eye on social media.

Sacred Grounds, Angel Wade Photography

Plant-based café and brunch spot

SACRED GROUNDS

From the hands that nurtured Exeter indie shop 'No Guts No Glory' comes plant-based café and brunch spot Sacred Grounds. Tuck into crispy waffles and vegan wraps, order a calming beetroot latte or an iced americano and spend your morning in the warm, light atrium of McCoy's Arcade. Look out for their regular live music sessions and feast nights as well!

ARTIGIANO

By day Artigiano serves an extensive coffee menu of flat whites and dirty chai lattes. But come evening this trendy coffee house is transformed into a stylish bar-space where you can sip on cocktails and catch live music performances.

Harry's Restaurant, Matt Austin Photography

PINK MOON

This Californian-inspired venue is seriously Instagrammable. Self-described as a 'Grab 'N' Go café, modern brunch space & social restaurant', Pink Moon is decked out with pastel pink walls, neon signage and white marble floors. There's an entire segment of their brunch menu devoted to how you like your eggs, as well as six different varieties of dirty fries on the all-day menu. Yes. Please.

GROW COFFEE HOUSE

The star of Grow is its sheltered outdoor decking area. Or maybe it's their coffee. Or perhaps it's their eco-friendly ethos? We can't actually decide! What we do know is that it's a bright and friendly spot to enjoy Devon roasted coffee and a pastry. Also attached to Grow is music shop Life Guitars Co. who lovingly revamp second-hand guitars back to glory.

RENDEZVOUS WINE BAR

This intimate basement wine bar is one of Exeter's best kept secrets. There's an exceptional wine list featuring over 60 suggestions from across the globe – as well as famous champagnes and local spirits – and an ever-changing menu of west country fare. Plus, in the summer months there's a peaceful, secluded garden to enjoy.

HARRY'S RESTAURANT

Harry's Restaurant is a stalwart of the Exeter foodie landscape. Established in 1993 by the Pounds family, this relaxed but beautifully outfitted restaurant has earned itself a glowing reputation. Between gourmet burgers and flat iron steaks, laidback brunches and a cookie dough dessert that's to die for, there really is something for everyone.

RED PANDA

Red Panda rustle up big, Asian street food flavours on Exeter's Gandy Street. Think fluffy bao buns and aromatic belly pork, made using fresh south west ingredients. Colourful dishes respect vegetables and give a kick to the tastebuds. You can also take home a jar of their crispy chilli sauce to recreate the magic at home (trust us, once you've tried it you'll be hooked).

THE CORK & TILE

Also tucked away on Gandy Street is The Cork and Tile. Serving up Portuguese cuisine and tapas, you can expect a sizeable menu of bite-sized dishes and authentic fare. All bases are covered, from crispy cod fritters to traditional Portuguese stews.

AL FARID

For a taste of Morocco, look no further than Al Farid. Overlooking Exeter's Cathedral Green, this laidback restaurant is lit by geomatic lanterns and festooned with colourful textiles. They offer the best meze around, alongside tempting tagines and shish platters – all washed down with authentic teas and traditional cocktails.

ON THE WATERFRONT

As the name suggests, this chilled out restaurant occupies an enviable waterside spot on Exeter Quay, overlooking the River Exe. It's 'go big or go home' when it comes to their famous 16-inch, dustbin lid pizzas. We're fans of the 'Crispy Duck' topping, but chilli heads need to try the 'Fiery Inferno' pizza.

VEG BOX CAFE

Elsewhere on Exeter's historic quayside, you'll find Veg Box Café – a vibrant café that's giving veggie and vegan food a thoroughly modern makeover. Its pink tiles and botanical-print cushions are matched by an equally vibrant menu, comprised of plant-based wraps, pancake stacks and Buddha bowls.

A vibrant café that's giving veggie and vegan food a thoroughly modern makeover.

Makers Mart

NgNg, Martha Simons Photography

HUTCH HOUSE PLANTS

Love plants? Do yourself a favour and drop into Hutch. Lush greenery bursts out from every corner and drips in strings from the ceiling. Purchase a leafy pal to improve the air quality of your home and add colour to a space – be it a stylish succulent, a fluffy-looking fern or a spiky cactus. Owners Rob and Frankie are real houseplant aficionados and are on hand to impart their expert advice.

SILVER LION JEWELLERS

Hammered silver jewellery, fiery precious stones, and quirky charms embellish the plush cushioned stands of Silver Lion Jewellers. Specialists in 9ct gold jewellery and unique pieces of silver, the shop offers a large selection of adornments that can be tailored to the wearer.

NO GUTS NO GLORY

Get your fix of houseplants, art prints and ceramics at this slick homeware shop on Exeter's Fore Street. Run by self-certified plant addicts, Alex and Martha, everything these guys sell is independently made, grown and built to last.

Lympstone Manor

exmouth

Lympstone Manor is a historic, Grade II listed Georgian manor house that has been transformed into a contemporary hotel for the 21st century. Chef patron Michael Caines is the man behind the manor, drawing on a wealth of experience to create an idyllic retreat by the picturesque Exe Estuary.

Each of the hotel's luxurious suites feature sumptuous beds, complimentary gin trays, Nespresso machines and ghd hair straighteners. What's more, the rooms are named after different birds native to the nearby estuary - a charming touch that weaves the hotel's interiors into the surrounding landscape.

Each of the hotel's three dining rooms are overseen by chef Caines, with award-winning menus showcasing modern European fine dining. Expect plenty of gels, delicate portions and avant-garde plating.

Maverick tip: A room at Lympstone Manor doesn't come cheap but their gorgeous new shepherd's huts are a touch more affordable and - we dare say - even more romantic!

———————

Lympstone Manor, Courtlands Lane
Exmouth, EX8 3NZ

www.lympstonemanor.co.uk

Redbrick Barn

Thorverton

Set in sixty acres of lush countryside, Redbrick Barn overlooks dramatic rolling hills and is perfectly located for exploring the many picturesque walks that Devon has to offer.

The venue itself benefits from a spacious open plan design, including a fully equipped kitchen and contemporary French doors leading out to a rustic outdoor dining area and well groomed courtyard. This al fresco space is the perfect retreat after long summer days well spent. Make the most of the gin bar and toast marshmallows over the fire pit as you sit back and while away the evening.

Maverick tip: If you're staying in and cooking, head to Exe Valley Farm Shop to stock up on essentials.

———————

Redbrick Barn, Pitt Farm
Thorverton, EX5 5LL

www.redbrickbarnandstudio.co.uk

Matthew Heritage Photography

Exe Valley Glamping

bickleigh

Exe Valley Glamping is a campsite made up of luxurious safari lodges that look out over the rolling green hills of mid-Devon. Each eco-conscious tent is equipped with all the amenities you need to have a relaxed weekend - like a kitchen, a refrigerator and a fire pit. This means you can camp in total comfort while still being immersed enough in nature to wake up to birdsong and huddle around the fire each evening. We love the idea of stoking up the barbecue and dining on your own private deck, as the sun goes down.

Maverick tip: Feeling active? Head to the Exe Estuary Trail. It's a 26 mile, mainly flat, cycle route and walkway, which runs around the entire Exe Estuary.

———————————

Exe Valley Glamping, Bickleigh
Tiverton, EX16 8RA

www.exevalleyglamping.com

HEAD EAST

East Devon is a patchwork of green fields, busy market towns and quaint coastal communities. It boasts more than its fair share of award-winning restaurants and is home to some of our favourite independent shops and businesses. Here's a little taste of what to expect from a visit:

BEER

There's something magical about the tiny coastal village of Beer. The high street and surrounding lanes look like they've been plucked straight from a bygone era, and its shingle beach, flanked by steep chalk cliffs on either side, is studded with colourful deck chairs and fishing boats. On a warm day, it's the perfect spot for a cool dip in the sea, or you can pull up a chair and tuck into a fresh crab sandwich right by the water.

Nearby, **Beer Quarry Caves** is a vast underground network of man-made caverns, carved out by centuries of quarrying for its famous Beer stone. First quarried by the Romans around 2,000 years ago, the stone from these caves has supplied materials for many historic landmarks including Exeter Cathedral, parts of Westminster Abbey, St Paul's Cathedral, the Tower of London and Windsor Castle!

AXMINSTER

Not too far from the town of Axminster is River Cottage. Made famous by Hugh Fearnley-Whittingstall's television series of the same name, this working farm and cookery school teaches back to basics courses where you can learn essential skills such as bread making, foraging and fish filleting.

After capturing the public's imagination on television, the 17th century River Cottage longhouse is now available to book as boutique accommodation. Sympathetically refurbished with the help of British manufacturers and designers, the rural retreat has been given a thoroughly 21st century makeover, while retaining many of its original farmhouse features.

HONITON

The market town of Honiton was once internationally famed for its lace and pottery industries. Today, it's widely regarded as the antiques capital of the South West and still boasts a largely independent high street.

Our first recommendation in Honiton has to be **Boston Tea Party.** BTP is technically a chain, but they serve some of the best brunches around. One of our favourite things about this café is the artwork on its walls. BTP Honiton curates its own artwork in collaboration with local artists, so you can purchase some affordable art along with your latte. They also have some excellent vegan and veggie options on their menu, including The Plant Burger, which is a solid 10/10.

When the sun is shining there's no better place to enjoy a cup of tea and a slice of cake than in **Toast Cafe & Patisserie**'s enchanting garden. Shaded by vines and home to songbirds and apple trees, this al fresco spot is seriously charming. Everything from their cupcakes to their crostini are made fresh, using ingredients from local suppliers.

Across the road from Toast Cafe & Patisserie you'll find **Fountain Antiques**. This shop is a regular haunt of vintage queen Kirsty Allsopp, and is an absolute Aladdin's cave of trinkets and antiques. It's very easy to spend a rainy afternoon rifling through piles of vintage fabrics and browsing their eclectic mix of furniture, artwork and Victoriana.

Come dinner time, the best place to be is **The Holt.** The food is uncomplicated and delicious, and there's something really warm and relaxing about the ambience. The restaurant is located upstairs, while downstairs you'll find a lively pub that pours pints of local ale, as well as their own brand of Otter Brewery beers.

Just outside Honiton town centre there's **Combe Garden Centre**, which is another one of our favourite places for coffee. They have a huge selection of houseplants here, as well as a contemporary café that serves great food, and a beautifully curated lifestyle store called **Velvet and Parade.**

OTTERY ST MARY

On the way to Sidmouth from Honiton, you'll drive past the town of Ottery St Mary: the famed birthplace of poet Samuel Taylor Coleridge and home to one of the craziest British traditions - 'Tar Barrels Night'. Every 5th November, the town comes alive with bonfire night festivities, chief of which is the burning barrels. In case the name wasn't literal enough for you, this is essentially a tradition where the townsfolk run through crowded streets with flaming barrels on their backs.

Don't miss **Joshua's Harvest Store** on your way into town. It's a seriously charming shop and cafe that specialises in homegrown produce and healthy living. We go here to stock up on spices, fresh veg, plant-based ingredients and eco-friendly cleaning products. Plus, they make a rather excellent latte and the best homity pie around.

Rusty Pig is undoubtedly the most popular restaurant in town. Self-described as a 'feasting house', lunch is a daily surprise – announced to you at your table – and dinner is a set menu made from the freshest ingredients available that day. Downstairs, there's a communal dining area complete with an open kitchen that allows you to interact with the chefs.

Joshua's Harvest Store

The Rusty Pig, Matt Austin Photography

Dukes - Matt Austin Photography

The Donkey Sanctuary

SIDMOUTH

The seaside town of Sidmouth was apparently author Jane Austen's staycation destination of choice, and unsurprisingly the town has retained much of its period charm. There are no flashy restaurants or retro amusements to be found on the esplanade, but you can stroll along the quaint Regency seafront and grab a cone of fish and chips to eat by the sea. The town is part of the world-famous Jurassic Coast which is a UNESCO World Heritage Site. Its iconic red cliffs are thousands of years old and bookend the town's sand and shingle beaches.

A strong contender for the best food in town is **Dukes.** This hotel, bar and restaurant is a popular spot and a true Sidmouth mainstay. Expect pub classics, fresh seafood, local meats, and some interesting plant-based options on their menu. They also host live music sessions throughout the summer season in their seafront beer garden.

A short walk from the town centre is **Connaught Gardens** - a beautiful collection of gardens with views of the entire esplanade and the sea. This outdoor venue was created in 1820 and a stroll through the grounds feels like a moment captured in time. The gardens are a popular location for free concerts and performances during the summer, and at low tide neighbouring **Jacob's Ladder Beach** is one of our favourite spots for sea swimming.

A short drive from Sidmouth is **The Donkey Sanctuary.** For over fifty years this charity has worked tirelessly to transform the lives of donkeys across the globe. A visit to the sanctuary lets you experience their work firsthand and gives you the opportunity to get up close to the rescue donkeys. Trust us when we say they're *seriously* cute, and your little ones will love this fun and educational day out.

BUDLEIGH SALTERTON & EXMOUTH

Budleigh Salterton boasts a long, pebbly seafront with colourful beach huts and a quiet high street. The average age of its residents is about seventy, but that's honestly one of the things that makes this town so charming. Grab yourself an ice cream cone and sit on the beach, or pop into **The Tipsy Merchant** for freshly caught lobsters and a bottle of wine to take home with you.

The town of Exmouth draws in a much younger crowd. Unlike East Devon's other beaches, it boasts two miles of golden sand and a wealth of rock pools. It's ideal for swimming and is filled with family-friendly amusements and places to eat.

Exmouth's new Sideshore development has plenty to offer, from water sports to dog-friendly cafés. **Mickeys Beach Bar** (left) was set up by award-winning local chef Michael Caines, who has created a laid-back, beachside atmosphere with a vibrant menu. There's also **Café Patisserie Glacerie** next door, which serves fresh coffee and some very Instagram-worthy pastries.

Also part of the development is **EDGE Watersports,** headed up by world champion kite surfer Steph Bridge and her family. They offer lessons and kit hire for everything from power kiting to SUP and beach yoga. There's also **Ella's Studio** - a creative space by eco-friendly artist Ella Slade, who paints vast seascapes onto canvas and reclaimed surfaces. Even her card machine is made from recycled ocean plastic!

Exmouth is also home to one of Devon's most unique offerings: **River Exe Cafe.** The only way to reach this popular venue is by water taxi, meaning it's located well off shore in the middle of the Exe Estuary. Few experiences can top the sensation of sipping cocktails and downing freshly shucked oysters on a floating restaurant with 360 sea views!

Lunch at River Exe Cafe

Mickeys Beach Bar & Restaurant

This historic town has plenty of charm &
lots to explore

TOPSHAM

A stone's throw from Exeter is one of our favourite places in all of Devon: Topsham. This historic town has plenty of charm and as you make your way down its quaint high street there are plenty of independent shops and eateries to explore.

For women's fashion, check out **Pea & Mint.** Garments are carefully chosen with an eye for detail and effortless style. There's also **Siena Boutique,** who curate well-made Scandinavian clothing and jewellery.

For the best coffee in town head to **Circle**. These guys know a thing or two about making a quality flat white and they're also big supporters of the Devon arts scene. Alongside awesome lattes, you'll find work by local artists and craftspeople, as well as a huge selection of houseplants.

At the quay, you have the choice to follow the road to the **Topsham Museum** or browse **Quay Antiques Centre -** a three-story warehouse packed to the rafters with over sixty dealers showcasing their antiques, collectables and curiosities.

Topsham's foodie credentials are top notch and for a small town it's awash with places to eat. **Sara's Petite Cuisine** sells delicious homemade pastries (do yourself a favour and try their Portuguese tarts) and **Denley's Essence of India** serves the best Indian cuisine in Devon. For fine dining, **The Galley** and **The Salutation Inn** are both fantastic options - though they do tend to be busy, so booking in advance is always recommended. If rustic dining and dirty burgers are more your bag, you ought to try **The Pig & Pallet**, where hearty meat platters, BBQ ribs and craft beer are the name of the game.

Of course, if you want to burn off all those calories, you can always rent a bike from **Route 2 Bikes** near the quay and cycle along the scenic **Exe Estuary Trail**.

Darts Farm

Topsham

Darts Farm is a vibrant, nationally award-winning farm shopping experience, with a working farm at its heart. As well as rearing their own herd of native Ruby Red Devon Cattle, each morning their team go out to the fields and hand-pick fresh seasonal fruit and veg for the food hall and onsite restaurants.

Their food hall is filled with hundreds of local and artisan suppliers; the best West Country cheeses, incredible artisan breads, local wines, craft beers, handmade chutneys and much more. It's not just about the food though. For home and lifestyle inspiration, they have the iconic specialist retailers; Fired Earth, AGA and Orange Tree.

Enjoy seasonal light lunches in the main restaurant, or pay a visit to their new restaurant and cidery, The Farm Table; where you can enjoy simple, seasonal ingredients, cooked over fire using wood and charcoal. For something a little sweeter, there's also their gelato and bean to bar chocolate area!

Darts Farm
Topsham, EX3 0QH

www.dartsfarm.co.uk

Darts Farm, Matt Austin Photography

The Five Bells

Clyst Hydon

Located in the sleepy village of Clyst Hydon,
The Five Bells Inn is a charming, thatched country pub
offering fine dining cuisine alongside classic dishes.
We love the cosy farmhouse atmosphere and the fact
that their bar is always well-stocked with real ales,
Devon ciders and local spirits.

It's easy to see why this venue has scooped a UK
Top 50 Gastropub award for two years running. Head
Chef Charlotte Vincent is a true artist in the kitchen.
She changes her menus in tandem with the seasons
and utilises the freshest locally grown ingredients
wherever possible. Make sure you check out their IG
page to swoon over her beautifully presented food!

Maverick tip: Get your friends together and book a
table to enjoy one of their hearty, award-winning
Sunday roasts - you won't regret it!

The Five Bells, Clyst Hydon
Cullompton, EX15 2NT

www.fivebells.uk.com

Ross Haywood, Well Seasoned PR

Otter Valley Field Kitchen

If small batch ice-creams, tangy sorbets and crispy stonebaked pizzas sound good, you'll probably love Otter Valley Field Kitchen as much as we do. Housed in a contemporary, glass-sided barn, they offer tasty food alongside stunning countryside views. All of their ice-cream is made using the milk from their own dairy herd, combined with the finest local ingredients.

Maverick tip: It's also smack bang on the A30, so it's the perfect pitstop if you're heading into Devon or Cornwall on holiday or driving up to London.

––––––––––––––

Otter Valley Field Kitchen,
Monkton, EX14 9sQN

www.ottervalleydairy.co.uk

THE PIG – at Combe

gittisham

You'll find The Pig - at Combe nestled in the beautiful
Otter Valley in the picture-perfect village of Gittisham.
This gorgeous Elizabethan country house hotel boasts
thirty bespoke rooms, lush country gardens,
a restaurant and sweeping valley views.

The Pig turns the traditional layout of a country house
on its head. Walking through the buildings historic
entrance takes you straight into the expansive bar
space at the hub of the hotel. Here you can take a seat
by the fireplace and sip on botanical cocktails inspired
by the onsite herb gardens. The interiors throughout
the hotel are to die for, with plenty of original features,
wood-panelled walls and sumptuous velvets.

Maverick tip: On a warm evening, nothing beats
kicking back with a cocktail at the converted Folly
building overlooking the lush grounds and valley.

———————————

The Pig - at Combe, Gittisham
Honiton, EX14 3AD

www.thepighotel.com/at-combe

Alex Middleton Photography

Finn Studio Photography

Glebe House

colyton

This relatively new addition to the Devonshire
hospitality scene is already making waves. Glebe House
is a guest house, restaurant and fifteen-acre
smallholding set in the heart of East Devon, in an area
of Outstanding Natural Beauty. This charming venue
boasts far-reaching views over the rolling hills of the
Coly Valley, and is only a short drive from the Jurassic
coast. Décor takes its cue from the lush, country
surroundings, with five guest bedrooms and an annexe
designed with bold use of colour and patterns, and
artistic details and murals throughout. The rooms have a
comfortable feel where guests will be greeted with
home-baked goods and refreshments on arrival.

Glebe House is as much a foodie retreat as it is a place
to stay. Inspired by Italy's agritourism (working farms with
restaurants, where guests can also stay), the venue has a
farm-to-table restaurant. It offers a regularly-changing
fixed menu, with each course designed according to the
season's harvest.

———————

Glebe House, Southleigh
Colyton, EX24 6SD

glebehousedevon.co.uk

Collate Interiors

Searching for something a little bit different? We'd like to introduce you to Collate - a homeware and interiors shop that is *truly* unique. From the vintage crockery down to its original black and white chequered floor, Collate blends together the traditional with the quirky. Its owner, Naomi, has a knack for bringing together quality pieces by small-scale South West makers and companies. It's the perfect shop for a slow browse through decorative, stylish antiques and new artisan gifts. You're guaranteed to find something that takes your fancy!

Maverick tip: Collate also has an Intagram page where you can keep up-to-date with new stock and get fabulous gift ideas - @collateinteriors

---

Collate Interiors, Trinty Square
Axminster, EX13 5AN

www.collateinteriors.com

Heron Farm

Honiton

Heron Farm is equal parts vineyard, farm and café, producing fabulous sparkling wines, as well as ciders and homegrown veggies. The fruits of the farm go straight into the sundaes, smoothies and cocktails that you'll find on the menu; which can all be sipped and enjoyed in their beautiful walled garden.

It's a peaceful spot for coffee in the sun, bordered by tulips and accompanied by the gentle trickle of running water. It's not just a romantic stop for wine lovers though, Heron Farm is family friendly with a play park and pygmy goats round the back.

Maverick tip: Heron Farm is best enjoyed on a sunny day. Grab a table outside and order one of their legendary sundaes.

Heron Farm, Weston
Honiton, EX14 3NZ

heron-farm.co.uk

Sunshine and Snow in Bideford

INDEPENDENT
SHOPPING

The excitement of visiting a new city can sometimes be dampened by the familiar sight of chain stores you have back at home. It's certainly incomparable to the joy of stumbling upon an indie shop after meandering up some promising yet higgledy-piggledy side streets. Thankfully, Devon is full of passionate people running independent businesses that breathe life into their towns and cities. Here are a few of our favourites...

GIFTS, INTERIORS & HOMEWARES

Sunshine and Snow, Bideford

This eye-catching boutique is a burst of vibrant colour on Bideford's Mill Street. They source artisan products from independent and local makers - stocking everything from homeware to fashion and stationery. Fun, original design is a running theme throughout Sunshine and Snow, so head here if you want your décor to double as art, or if you just want to find a pair of really good sunglasses.

Distinctly Living, Dartmouth

Home and kitchen store Distinctly Living is in beautiful Dartmouth, but sources its interiors from all over Europe. The small family-run shop accommodates a wide variety of styles, focusing on high quality products that add instant character to a room. There's lots to explore, from elegant carafes to lobster themed salt & pepper shakers!

Mor Gifts and Interiors, Lynmouth

The edge of Exmoor might be an unexpected place to find quirky home furnishings, but stumble across Mor Gifts and Interiors and you'll find just that. The shop is awash with home furnishings that will bring personality, colour and a dash of humour to any room. Some items border on kitsch, but that's all part of the charm.

Me and East, Totnes

This cool, slate shop overlooks Rotherfold Square in Totnes. Owner Chloe O'Brien's appreciation for the handmade is clear, as she sources and sells a pretty collection of tactile ceramics, hand-poured candles, unique jewellery and bath oils. Basically, Me and East stocks all sorts of things you'll want to pick up and take home with you - all made by small UK businesses and independent craftspeople.

A pretty collection of tactile ceramics, handpoured candles, unique jewellery

Nest, Topsham

Nest, Topsham

As its name suggests, Nest offers a curated collection of gifts and accessories to make your home a relaxing and joyous space. On its shelves you'll find everything from handmade chocolates to essential oil body wash, soft alpaca wool socks, and calming pillow mist. They also stock preloved clothes, pretty stationery and uplifting homeware to embellish your own nest with. Find their little teal shop on Topsham's Fore Street.

Dotty Home Interiors, Sidmouth

Our favourite thing about Dotty Home Interiors is the dreamy, pastel colour palette, which graces everything from their velvet cushion covers to their striped dinner candles. From the seaside town of Sidmouth, they present a sophisticated edit of homewares, gifts and lifestyle accessories - all lovingly curated from brands across the UK and Europe.

FOOD & DRINK

Wildmoor Delicatessen, Bovey Tracey

Wildmoor Delicatessen sits on the cusp of Dartmoor, in the town of Bovey Tracey. Their glowing deli counter of British and European cheeses makes them a haven for foodies to flock to. Staff can also help create the perfect cheeseboard with all the accompaniments, including, most importantly, the wine. On a warm evening, we recommend sinking a good glass of red with a deli board in Wildmoor's 'wine courtyard'.

Barrel and Still, Kingsbridge

This friendly wine and spirits shop has knowledgeable staff who will help you select the perfect tipple. They stock a varied and interesting selection of distinct spirits and wines to sample, including a few locally made gems like Dartmoor whiskeys and Salcombe Gin. Their interesting and unique bottles means that they work well as gifts too!

Johns of Instow, Instow

This independent deli and café serves homemade and local produce, freshly baked treats and good coffee. You'll find the deli in the heart of the seaside village Instow, overlooking the idyllic River Torridge and just a short walk from sandy Westward Ho! It's a friendly community hub which favours artisan produce and offers brilliant cheese and charcuterie boxes.

Relish Lifestyle (left & above)

Relish Home, Kingsbridge

Relish Home is run by experienced husband and wife team, Amy and Shaun, who are skilled in both interior design and craftsmanship; talents they use to revive antiques and create bespoke interiors. Expect a satisfying blend of modern and rustic home décor, and characterful pieces with lots of texture at their Kingsbridge shop. Their main draw, if you're interested in sustainable living, is their lovingly restored reclaimed furniture.

The Forest and Co, Dartington

The Forest and Co. showroom is stocked with modern classics, pieces which are comforting, elegant, understated and rustic, from Devon craftspeople and over the globe. Luxurious patterned textile quilts, fluffy sheepskins and overall indulgent interiors that inspire you to light a candle and snuggle up on a velvet sofa. Last time we checked these guys we're on a brief showroom hiatus (thanks Covid!) but their range is available to shop online.

Apparel & accessories with an ethical conscience

Sancho's, Exeter

CLOTHING & ACCESSORIES

Sancho's, Exeter

Located on Exeter's Fore Street, Sancho's is owned and run by Kalkidan Legesse, a Black Ethiopian British woman, who is passionate about ethical fashion, equality and sustainability. Inside you'll find a curated collection of apparel and accessories with an ethical conscience, made in fair trade conditions with organic, recycled and regenerative materials. Garments are wonderfully tactile and designed to stand the test of time.

Busby & Fox

With brick and mortar shops in Salcombe, Exeter, Totnes and Kingsbridge there's plenty of opportunities to pop into clothing and lifestyle store, Busby & Fox. Brimming with evergreen pieces that are relaxed and versatile, shop here for soft, comfortable wardrobe staples that layer well. It's perfect for those who have a relaxed, effortless style.

HEALTH & BEAUTY

Soapdaze, Exeter

Soapdaze sell grown-up, vegan soaps in scents like Ginger & Mandarin, Coffee & Raw Cacao and Cedarwood & Grapefruit. They're all handcrafted in Devon and sold in eco-friendly packaging (you can take soaps home unwrapped for added eco brownie points). Soapdaze also stocks organic refillable makeup, skincare, candles and bodycare. Take your time in their Exeter store - browsing through the swirling designs and fragrant scents on thick chunks of soap feels a bit like perusing through a sweet shop!

Andrew Dominic Furniture produces signature collections and custom commissions for renowned interior designers, architects and private clients across the globe.

Known for uncompromising dedication to quality, detail and authentic design – their offering is both timeless and elegant.

Each piece is handcrafted, using age-old methods and time-honoured skills, from sustainably sourced hardwood with natural oil finishes – and they're close to creating a zero-carbon footprint in their workshops.

andrewdominicfurniture.com | studio@andrewdominicfurniture.com | 01548 856871

  @andrewdominicfurniture

Pursuit of Adventure

Rachæl Brown discovers some of Devon's most
adventurous activities for thrill seekers and
adrenaline junkies.

RIB Rides in Salcombe

For a high-speed, exhilarating boat trip with lashings of
sea spray, Adventure South offer RIB rides along the
South Devon coastline. Get your heart racing as you
tear off around the waters near Salcombe, strapped in
with a bunch of family or friends, surrounded by
stunning coastal scenery.

Surfing in Croyde

The South West is home to some of the best surfing
beaches in the country, so we have to recommend a
couple of lessons with 'Surfing Croyde Bay'- even if
you're just aiming to stand up once. Spend the
morning honing your technique in the water, then step
out refreshed onto the golden sand.

North Devon Coasteering

Coasteering in North Devon

Xtreme Coasteering can take you out to a number of spots on the rugged North Devon coastline. The idea is to traverse across rock faces and climb sea cliffs with the bracing swell of the Atlantic crashing against you, culminating in a courageous jump into the ocean!

SUP in Ilfracombe

Ilfracombe's jade waters and dramatic cliff faces provide the perfect backdrop for paddleboarding. Drifting along, not only can you discover secluded coves that are hidden if on foot, but if you book with Active Escape you can also explore private coastline. The team offer individual SUP sessions, as well as family and giant party SUP for bigger groups.

Kayak in South Devon

Nothing beats a relaxing kayak through hidden coves and secret inlets at sunset. Sea Kayak Devon offer full or half-day guided trips around South Devon taking you to rocky islets, beaches and sea caves, putting you eye-to-eye with marine wildlife.

Gorge Scrambling on Dartmoor

It's not just plunging into pools - 'gorge scrambling' involves clambering over rocks, sliding down flumes and climbing through waterfalls. There are spots for wading through wild rivers all over Dartmoor, but to have the safety and experience of a guide, 'Adventure Okehampton' runs family-friendly trips.

Spy Seals on Lundy Island

Playful grey seals reside in the waters around rugged Lundy Island. Dive down into their underwater world for a peek into their secret lives below the waves. If they are feeling confident, these inquisitive animals may want to interact with you. Such a unique experience sells out fast, so book early.

Mountain Biking in Haldon Forest

Mountain bike down slim, rocky trails that snake through the green woodland of Haldon Forest near Exeter. Bikes are available to rent on-site but it's worth waiting for a quieter day if you can, as routes can sometimes get busy at the weekend. There are many different trails and tracks, so choose whichever difficulty matches your experience.

Fairy folk

LEGENDS OF DARTMOOR

ILLUSTRATIONS BY ELIN MANON

With its imposing tors and wild woodland, Dartmoor is as breathtaking as it is vast and unknowable. For centuries it has inspired writers and artists with its tales of ghostly apparitions, witches, and curious happenings. Here are a few of our favourite local legends...

THE FAIRY FOLK

Throughout Devon and Cornwall stories of fairies have endured for centuries. These tiny creatures are rumoured to be seen only in the twinkling of an eye, or between one blink and the next. They're highly elusive creatures, who are fiercely protective of their privacy, and have been known to blind those who spy on them.

All different kinds of fairy feature in British folklore, from the grotesque Spriggans native to Cornwall, to the beautiful Fairy Aristocrats described in fifteenth century ballads. Most descriptions of fairies depict them as fair little people, who are well-proportioned and imagined in clothes that mimic the natural landscape. While some fairies are said to have dainty little wings, most rely on magic incantations to fly or ride on ragwort stalks. Mischievous by nature, even the most innocent looking fairy is said to be dangerous. So, if you happen upon the fae when hiking on the moors, be careful to watch your step!

SPEAK OF THE DEVIL

Sightings of the Devil are remarkably common on Dartmoor; though accounts claim that he often appears in the guise of a huntsman or an evil rider.

A particularly well known account is tied to a historic thunderstorm that devastated Widdecombe Church on Sunday 21st October, 1638. The story starts in the small village of Poundsgate. That morning, church-dodging folk were busy exchanging stories and sinking tankards of ale at The Tavistock Inn. Suddenly, an eerie silence fell over the surrounding countryside and the clattering of hooves on cobbles could be heard approaching the inn.

A feeling of unease washed over the patrons as a tall figure, shrouded in dark robes and seated upon a high horse, approached the inn. As the figure came to a stop, the locals did not recognise the shadowy stranger, whose jet-black steed snorted and pounded the ground impatiently. From under the shadowy hood emerged a voice like nails on a chalkboard: "Fetch me a flagon of cider," it demanded. "Quickly, for I have a terrible thirst."

With shaking hands the landlady delivered his order, which he seized from her, before throwing two silver coins at her feet. He drained the tankard with a long, hissing gulp before tossing it aside and riding off again on the Widecombe road.

Shortly after, the rider arrived at Widecombe Church. Here he rode onto the roof and tethered his steed to the pinnacle tower. The local congregation were already inside, and peering through a gap in the ceiling, he spied a young boy asleep in the back row. It was common knowledge that those who fell asleep in church could fall into the hands of evil. So the rider - who had been the Devil all along -

seized his opportunity and swooped on the boy. Seizing him by his neck, he dragged the child from his pew and flung him across the saddle of his horse. In his haste to ride off with his prey, the devil broke the pinnacle of the tower, which came thundering down onto the remaining congregation. Thankfully, no one was killed; but many people were injured and the boy was never seen again...

Back in Poundsgate, the locals heard the rider pass again. This time they had drawn the windows tightly shut and held a collective breath as he went by. Only when the sound of hooves was gone did they breathe a sigh of relief and dare to look outside. Calm had returned to the moors, but when the landlady glanced at the silver coins the horseman had given her, she discovered that they had been transformed into withered leaves.

"It must have been the pixies who did this," she said. "It was an act of kindness. They knew this money was evil and so they changed it".

The evil rider

VIXANA THE WITCH

Somewhere between Tavistock and Princetown, you'll come across a particularly unusual tor that bears an uncanny resemblance to a woman's head. Vixen Tor - also known as Sphinx Tor - is a stony formation shrouded in mystery. Many centuries ago, the landmark was allegedly home to a witch named 'Vixana', who lived alone in a dark and cavernous cave at the base of the tor.

Vixana had an evil reputation among the locals, not least because of her terrifying appearance. She was said to have been taller than most men and as thin as a rake. The witch's long black hair hung down around her knees and her pale, sallow skin was drawn tight over her bones. As a malevolent soul, Vixana would take pleasure from the suffering of others and within her magical repertoire was the ability to conjure up a thick fog to trap anyone who would pass by her home.

Each day, Vixana would climb to the top of her tor and survey the boggy landscape for potential victims. When a lost traveller wandered too closely to her lair, she would summon the eerie fog and watch as they lost sight of their path. The most unfortunate among them would stumble into a deep, syrupy bog, and sink beneath the surface with the evil cackling of Vixana ringing in their ears.

But not all accounts of Vixana are so damning. During the Bronze Age, men buried their dead in the shadow of the Vixen Tor, making it a place of sacred significance. An alternative legend paints Vixana as a benevolent spirit who keeps watch over the land and the dead. In such accounts, the beautiful Vixana can take the form of a striking red vixen - which makes sense when you realise that foxes have always been considered creatures of the underworld, who spend their winters sheltering beneath the ground in earth dens. Dubbed 'The Mother of the Moor', Vixana keeps watch over the land, provides protection to travellers and offers peaceful entry to the Otherworld.

ANDREW DOMINIC
FURNITURE

Andrew Dominic Furniture is a brand that is synonymous with quality and authenticity. Their signature collections and custom, hand-crafted commissions have garnered the attention of renowned interior designers, architects and private clients across the globe; and it it's easy to see why. The business draws on over a decade of craftsmanship to produce furniture that is both timeless and elegant. The opening of their second workshop, here in the South Hams, ushers in an exciting new chapter for Andrew Dominic Furniture, that began in Cape Town, South Africa, more than ten years ago. We caught up with the man behind the brand to learn more about his creative process and the appeal of Devon's south coast...

Andrew, when did you discover your passion for furniture design?

I enjoyed dabbling in woodwork from a young age, in my Dad's workshop and tinkering with maintenance on our family boat, growing up here in Devon. But it was later on that I discovered my desire to pursue a career in woodwork, whilst working on classic yachts in the Mediterranean. As a crew member I got involved in the interior refit of a 100m classic Schooner when we were based in Gloucester Docks, which opened my eyes to new possibilities. At the time I was very set on boats and the sea, but I knew essentially that I had to follow a creative path to have a fully satisfying career.

What aspects of design do you find most exciting?

The refinement phase, where I move forward and backwards with possibilities to ultimately find the resting place in the design. Often this is reached after making a piece a couple of times - because I naturally design by making. I really enjoy the creative process of working through ideas to get to the essence of a design. But of course, it's also hard not to get excited when a large delivery of raw timber arrives at my workshop!

How would you describe your aesthetic?

It's always been my intention to try to let t he beauty of wood be part of the design. At both our workshops, here in Devon and in Cape Town, we produce handcrafted pieces using age-old methods and time-honoured skills.

Which item of furniture from your collection best represents your brand?

Our Noah Drinks Cabinet (above), because it embodies our style of design and encapsulates our process of designing to refine and resolve; it is elegant but importantly it is also a practical, functional piece. I liken it to a classic yacht. It has timeless lines but is first and foremost about functionality, and all the detailed design solutions are concealed within an aesthetically pleasing form. I like to think we've captured that essence in the design of this cabinet.

What role does your wife Susie play in the day-to-day running of the business?

My wife Susie has believed in me the whole way, sharing the load and challenges of every step. She's more of an idealist where I am a realist, and as business partners I've appreciated our symbiotic decision making. With a degree in Graphic Design & Photography, she manages the brand development and website, along with most of the daily client communications. The business wouldn't be where it is today without her!

How have you ensured that the business remains both responsible and sustainable?

We're very aware that our industry has a direct impact on the environment, so we see it as our responsibility to make sure that our impact is a positive one. Being responsible and working sustainably is at the heart of our business, but we believe that sustainability isn't a destination – it's a process of being aware, staying open to learning and improving. We only use select hardwoods from sustainably managed forests, as close to the source as possible, and natural non-toxic oil with water-based finishes and glues. We're working towards making our workshops zero-carbon and manage our wood waste by composting it, taking it back to the natural life cycle.

Do your Devon and your South African commissions differ in any way?

Not hugely, but then again, it's still early days. We are already starting to see more interior designers requesting bespoke items here in the UK, so it could possibly be that this personalised and bespoke approach will be an area of difference - in South Africa the driving force of our custom comes primarily from our core collections.

What led you to return to Devon?

To slow down, have more space and time; to return to the wholesome, calm of the Devon coast and countryside. For myself and our three young children.

Discover more about Andrew Dominic Furniture and explore their collection at *www.andrewdominicfurniture.com*

FELTED SHEEPSKINS

If you're anything like us, at one point or another you've found yourself lusting after an authentic sheepskin rug for your living room. But the initial lure of these rustic textiles is often accompanied by a tinge of guilt for the sheep who's supplied it. If that scenario rings any bells, then you'll love our next artisan interview. From her smallholding and studio on Dartmoor, Rosie Anderson crafts totally unique, cruelty-free 'sheepskins'. These sensational felted 'skins' allow you to nab yourself a gorgeous new throw without feeling *sheepish* about its provenance...

"I have a smallholding near St Giles on the Heath, where I make felted sheepskins along with my mum.** These look just like real sheepskins but are made only from the shorn fleece, so no animals are harmed in the process. Sometimes people call them 'vegetarian sheepskins'.

I had always loved the look of sheepskins but hated the idea of what they actually are. I was visiting an aunt on the Isle of Arran in Scotland (she is an amazing felt maker) and she had a felted sheepskin that she had made. Several years later, when I finally had my own flock of sheep, I was wondering what I could do to add value to their wool and making felted sheepskins just made sense!

We love to use all different breeds and crossbreeds of sheep; the different textures and colours keep it really interesting. Fleece quality can vary hugely, even within the same breed, so we have to hand-pick all of the fleeces we use. We love to use Masham wool as it has the most amazing curls, and Dartmoors have wonderful texture, but equally we have made beautiful fleeces from the most unexpected cross breeds.

I have around forty sheep on our farm which I keep for wool. We have a really mixed little flock and our most recent edition is a Valais Blacknose ram called Freddy, who will hopefully add interesting quality to our wool. We really believe in farming in a wildlife friendly way, so we have to keep our sheep numbers low because we don't graze all of our land all of the time. We worked with Devon Wildlife Trust to create species-rich wildflower meadows which are amazing. In the summer they are buzzing with all sorts of insects and butterflies, but the sheep aren't allowed to graze on them during the growing season.

I'd heard of Rebecca Hosking's Forever Flock because of her farming technique, which really works in harmony with nature. Over the last few years, we've worked a lot with Rebecca and her partner Dave – they know what we are looking for and manage their flock in a way that fits with our ethos, but also in a way that produces really good quality fleece and wool.

We were so lucky to be taught by my aunt. She came all the way to Devon and spent a week with us teaching us the basic techniques. From there, we have adapted and tweaked the method to find a process that works consistently. There's been lots of trial and error to get to the point we are at now!

Felted sheepskins and regular sheepskins are so different that it's difficult to think of them as a similar product. Ultimately, it comes down to what's important to you as an individual. Unlike the tanning process of regular sheepskins, our process does not involve any harsh chemicals, as we only use olive oil soap and saved rainwater; this also means what we do is sustainable and environmentally friendly. Another thing to keep in mind is that *all* real sheepskins are a by-product of the meat industry, and the wonderful thing about felted sheepskins is that the sheep are still happily living their lives!

Each felted sheepskin takes about a day in total to produce. It can very much depend on the fleece we are working with, as some require more time than others. The felting process is wet and messy, and after they've dried - which can take several days - the finishing process involves grooming and perfecting the fleece. We do offer a limited number of workshops to learn the techniques. They last a whole day and it's quite physical work, as you're on your feet all day, but the great thing about them is you get to take home your very own rug.

A felted sheepskin is an investment for life, because felt is incredibly strong and long-lasting. They don't really require much upkeep – I usually just give mine a shake to fluff them up and a soft brush from time to time.

We love to use all different
breeds and crossbreeds of sheep

I love my studio space. It sits at the top of one of our barns and has big windows that overlook the countryside. The studio is stuffed full of fleeces, all stored in paper bags, and I have a big table in the middle where I work. In the corner is an old Butler sink reclaimed from a friend's garden, and there is always a dog asleep in the corner keeping me company. It also has no internet signal - so when I'm working I can't be distracted!

I definitely have a favourite sheep! It's hard not to because some sheep really do make a connection with you. I'd have to choose Ted; he is a Blue Texel ram and is just the friendliest, most chilled out guy you could imagine. He always wants attention and he always gets it. I just adore him. Rebecca from the Forever Flock also knows all of her sheep by name and is a great photographer, so not only does she provide fleeces but also beautiful portraits of their unique characters.

I'd say the best thing about living in Devon is being surrounded by nature and having space. I grew up here, so it feels like the right place to be. I feel lucky every day to live in this part of the world and be raising my kids here. You are never that far from an amazing beach or a beautiful moor. My favourite place in Devon is slap bang in the middle of my wildflower meadows when then are in full bloom, trying to catch crickets with my kids. Also anywhere on the South West Coast Path which is just out of this world.

To learn more about Felted Sheepskins and purchase their products, head to: feltedsheepskins.co.uk

SURF'S UP!

BROAD SANDS

Broad Sands is North Devon's worst kept secret. Secluded by wild cliffs that are thick with luscious greenery, the beach opens up to a stunning view of turquoise water. On a sunny day it has a, dare I say, tropical feel, but it's a shingley beach so don't expect golden sands!

CELLARS BEACH

Cellars Beach is a little cove off the River Yealm. You can park at Noss Mayo and embark on the 35 minute trundle through pretty riverside woodland down to the beach. If the tide is high, the beach is reduced to a large rock, surrounded by see-to-the-bottom water - great for a cool plunge before drying off like a lizard in the sun. It's important to check the tide times though, as water can creep into part of the car park at high tide.

EAST PORTLEMOUTH

East Portlemouth is a smooth sandy beach with clear waters and a relaxed feel, making it perfect for sunbathing and a quiet dip. From its golden shore you can admire the white houses of Salcombe, the boats bobbing in the estuary and the curve of sweeping green cliffs that keep the sands relatively sheltered. The easiest way to get to East Portlemouth is by ferry from Salcombe, to avoid narrow roads and full car parks. Once you're on the beach, find a quiet cove that catches the sunset.

Above & Previous Page: Westward Ho! Jack Levick Photography

WESTWARD HO!

You can catch some gorgeous, soft sunsets from Westward Ho! thanks to the wide open skies along its extensive stretch of sand. Surf-wise, the beach is beginner friendly with a hire shop in the town, but if the bracing waves of the Atlantic aren't for you there is also a sea pool for a gentle dip. Alternatively, follow the coast round to Appledore: a charming fishing village on the River Torridge.

LADRAM BAY

Ladram Bay is a beautifully curving pebble beach to the east of Budleigh Salterton, characterised by its dramatic, red sea stacks. It's fun to kayak or swim out to these sandstone islands, weave around them, discover caves to climb through and ledges to clamber on, or simply to see these wonderful towers from a different perspective.

WOODY BAY

Although Woody Bay is remote - on a crinkle of Exmoor's rugged coastline - and has a steep climb down to the sea, it makes up for it with lovely views and a sense of exclusivity. Clamber the boulders or lounge on rocks to soak up the sun, admire the small waterfall or take advantage of its giant rock pool for safe swimming. It's a stoney beach, often strewn with seaweed, so you might want to bear that in mind...

Hartland Quay, ASC Photography

HARTLAND QUAY

Hartland Quay is known for its remarkable scenery, often featuring crashing waves, but always with towering cliffs and giant italic rock formations that jut into the sea. As you walk down from the top of the headland, there are far-reaching views of the North Devon coastline and on a good day you can surf and bathe against its dramatic backdrop.

LANNACOMBE BEACH

The epitome of unspoilt rugged beauty, Lannacombe feels wild but has soft sand. It's a quieter beach, tucked away and bordered by rock formations that reveal seaweed pools to explore when the tide goes out. This is a peaceful part of South Devon's coastline that welcomes dogs all year round.

Croyde at Sunset, Ian Woolcock Photography

BLACKPOOL SANDS

Blackpool Sands is a Blue Flag award-winning beach, backed by lush rolling hills, evergreens and scented pines. Despite its deceptive name, it's actually a shingle beach, named after the local town of Blackpool (near Dartmouth). Located in a sheltered bay, the beach is privately managed and kept in immaculate condition. It even boasts its own café 'Venus Beach', where you can enjoy peaceful breakfasts and light lunches with some stunning sea views.

CROYDE BEACH

Croyde is one of North Devon's most popular beaches, with its fine golden sands and even finer surf. Surrounded by sand dunes and green rolling hills, this laidback beach is perfect for families and surfers alike. Croyde Village is just a short distance away, so when you're done on the beach you can head for a pint at one of its popular local pubs.

183

Easy Recipes

Photography by Matt Austin

For the past six years, chef Chris Onions has been serving up rustic feasts at The Old Dairy Kitchen in East Devon. His colourful dishes and modest, ethical cooking have earned him quite the reputation. So, we asked him to whip up some vibrant, easy-to-follow recipes using fresh Devon ingredients...

Chickpea, Nettle & Wild Garlic Fritters

SERVES 4

For the fritters

150g nettle puree (method below)

1 finely chopped onion

2 large handfuls of wild garlic

200g chickpea flour

600ml warm water

Salt

2 tsp finely chopped rosemary

2 tbsp grated hard goats cheese

1 tbsp olive oil

Oil for frying

For the nettle puree

1 small bin bag of freshly picked nettles

TO MAKE THE FRITTERS

1. Warm the olive oil in large, heavy bottomed pot, add the onion and fry gently for 5 mins - without adding any colour. Add the rosemary and the water and bring to the boil.

2. Slowly sieve the chickpea flour into the pan of boiling liquid, stirring continuously. Add the salt and keep stirring until the mixture comes back to the boil.

3. Reduce the heat and cook for a further 40 mins, stirring continuously as if making polenta. Take care, the mixture will become very thick and can stick to the bottom of the pot. While the chickpeas are cooking, line a tray with a sheet of greaseproof paper and set to one side.

4. When the chickpea mixture begins to come away from the sides of the pot and has a fine texture, add the cheese and roughly chopped wild garlic and pour into the tray to set and cool.

5. Once set, slice to your desired shape and size. Heat a pan of sunflower oil to 180C and deep fry the slices until crisp and golden. Drain and serve immediately.

TO MAKE THE NETTLE PUREE

Nettles are best picked in early spring or after they have been cut back and new shoots appear before the plants go to seed. Pick the top four to six leaves using some gloves, and as with all wild food make sure you are certain you know what you are picking!

1. Bring a large pan of salted water to the boil. Once boiling add the nettles and cook for 3 mins, remove the nettles from the pan and plunge into ice cold water to stop them cooking and to keep their brilliant green colour. After a minute, drain off the water and squeeze off any excess water from the nettles.

2. Add the nettles to the food processor and puree for a few minutes to achieve a smooth paste.

White Fish, Endive & Gooseberry

SERVES 4

400g white fish fillet

50g cane sugar

50g salt

150g gooseberries, juiced

½ lemon, juiced

1 large head of endive or chicory

1 tbsp olive oil

1 tbsp finely chopped chives

1 tsp finely chopped mint

1 elderflower head (optional)

This dish works well with a whole variety of white fish, from plaice to pollock, and you can also introduce cockles, clams or raw scallops. What's most important is that you find the best quality, sustainably fished produce from local day boats. As with the garden, the fish all have seasons, so you can play about with the other ingredients too. We substitute gooseberries for crab apples and chicory in the winter.

1. Begin by curing the fish; combine the salt and sugar to make your cure. Once mixed, sprinkle generously all over the fish and let it cure for 30 mins. Once cured, carefully rinse off the salt mixture and pat the fish dry with a clean towel.

2. Now cut the fish into 1cm cubes and place in a glass or plastic bowl. Add the gooseberry and lemon juice, cover and place in the fridge for 1 hour.

3. Cut the bottom from your endive and give the leaves a quick wash if needed. Lay the leaves out on your serving dish, cup side facing up. Remove the fish from the fridge and add the chives, mint and olive oil, mixing very carefully. Taste for seasoning and add a little salt if needed.

4. Spoon the mixture into the endive shells and sprinkle over some elderflower heads if you have them. Serve immediately.

Grilled Rhubarb, Mead & Elderflower Cream

SERVES 6

For the elderflower cream

4 egg yolks

120g sugar

60g plain flour

500ml whole organic milk

5 heads of fresh elderflower

300ml organic double cream

For the grilled rhubarb

2 tbsp honey

150ml mead (or water)

½ vanilla pod

750g rhubarb

TO MAKE THE ELDERFLOWER CREAM

1. Start by making a pastry cream. Whisk together the egg yolks and sugar for 30 seconds, add the flour and whisk for a further 20 seconds. Set to one side.

2. Bring the milk and elderflower heads to the boil in a saucepan. Once boiled, pour through a sieve onto the egg mixture, pressing the heads gently to extract as much flavour as possible and whisk to combine.

3. Return your mixture to the saucepan and cook on a medium heat, whisking continuously for 2 mins until the mixture is thick and shiny. Transfer the mixture into a bowl and loosely cover with a little greaseproof paper, place in the fridge and cool completely.

4. Once cool, transfer 300g of the pastry cream to a separate bowl and whisk for a few seconds to loosen up, add the double cream and continue whisking until you achieve a whipped cream consistency. Store in the fridge until needed.

TO MAKE THE GRILLED RHUBARB

1. Add the honey and mead to a small saucepan, then split the vanilla pod and scrape out the seeds and combine with the honey and mead. Bring to a simmer and remove from the heat.

2. Give the rhubarb a quick wash and split each stick into 4 long pieces. Grill the rhubarb strips on the barbecue or griddle pan for a few minutes to achieve a light char. Transfer them to a tray and pour over the mead mixture whilst still warm. Let the mixture rest for an hour before serving.

3. To serve, place a large spoonful of the elderflower cream onto your serving dishes and lay the rhubarb on top, spoon over the sweet and sour mead syrup.

Notes

Notes